The lost zodiac

of

Rudolf Steiner

*Exploring the four sets of zodiac images
designed by Rudolf Steiner*

Adrian Anderson   Ph.D.

Threshold Publishing, Australia 2016
www.rudolfsteinerstudies.com

Distributed by Dennis Jones P/L - Port Campbell Press
Bayswater VIC
Australia

ISBN 978-0-9941602-6-3 hardback
ISBN 978-0-9941602-5-6 paperback

Contents

Illustrations

Foreword

Whilst walking along a street in Dornach one delightful spring day in the early 1980's, I came across an 'Antiquariat', a second-hand bookstore which specialized in anthroposophical material. Inside, I noticed an old Almanac or Star Calendar, from 1947. It caught my eye, and on opening it, I stood transfixed, staring at some small black and white photos showing twelve amazing images of the zodiac, designed by Rudolf Steiner. The images themselves were surrounded by images of the four signs of the zodiac. The Almanac reported that it was painted onto the ceiling of the main room of Anthroposophical Centre in Stuttgart by Baroness Imma von Eckhardtstein, after discussions with Rudolf Steiner. But it did not survive when the building was destroyed, in 1937.

I had found yet another treasure amongst the people of Central Europe from the heritage of Rudolf Steiner's life-work, so tragically cut short by his early death in 1925. I was to spend several more years searching for such treasures in Europe, from which in later years, it was my intention, after decades of preparation, to create books offering insights into anthroposophy. I happily paid the one Mark (about one dollar) and carefully put the journal aside, so that in the future, when I was back in the southern hemisphere, this gift from the spiritual world could live again.

Anthroposophy was defined by Rudolf Steiner on one occasion as "A path of knowledge that leads the spiritual in the human being to the spiritual in the cosmos." His anthroposophical teachings were in many ways an embodiment of this statement. The most vivid graphic expressions of this statement are surely the several series of new images for the zodiac which he designed, and which we shall explore: of these zodiac symbols, the ones painted on the ceiling of the anthroposophical Centre in Stuttgart, in 1911-12 are the most striking. They offer the spiritual seeker with a magnificent series of images, deeply evocative of cosmic forces active in humanity.

Although the painting was destroyed in the late 1930's, these images are once again available here, because black & white photographs were taken of them in the 1920's. This zodiac has been re-created, in its original colour so far as possible, allowing people to again contemplate the zodiac energies, which speak to us in powerful, evocative imagery of our link to the cosmos. In addition, the three other sets of zodiac images designed by Rudolf Steiner are also presented and explained.

A good quality print of this Stuttgart zodiac is available through a link on the author's website: www.rudolfsteinerstudies.com

Introduction: The four different series of zodiac images designed by Rudolf Steiner

We shall be exploring in detail the Stuttgart zodiac, and also the three other sets of zodiac images designed by Rudolf Steiner. Undoubtedly the most impressive of these four sets of zodiac images is the one from Stuttgart. It arose as the result of a conversation between Rudolf Steiner and the painter, as he and a small group of friends, accompanied Marie Steiner on a recuperative holiday to a small town of Portoros near Trieste in Italy on the Adriatic coast, in 1911. This impressive work of art was consequently painted in 1911-12 with great skill on to the cupola ceiling of the room in Stuttgart. During the years 1911-1915 Rudolf Steiner also created three other sets of new images for the zodiac. The images presented in this Stuttgart painting were similar to the series of drawings which were published in a book produced in 1912, called *The Calendar of 1912/13*. It was again Baroness Eckhardtstein who drew the images for this publication; some of which resemble those on the ceiling of the Stuttgart building. In this book, Rudolf Steiner also published his Soul Calendar for the first time, together with a calendar for each day of the year, in which was entered the birth or death dates of famous and significant people and some major events in history.

Also in 1912, Rudolf Steiner approached a gifted painter, Anna May, who was a deeply devout anthroposophist, with the idea of her creating a huge esoteric painting which would speak to the viewer with images of great power, about the secrets of esoteric Christianity and the high initiate behind the medieval Rosicrucian movement, known as Christian Rosencreutz. This painting also contains small images of the zodiac, as just one of its many themes. The only colour photo taken of the painting about 1914, and consequently published as a colour print in 1975, has small zodiac figures. Sadly, this huge, esoteric work of art was destroyed in World War II. We shall briefly explore its images later in the book. This vitally important painting, now unattainable, will be available again in a book by this author, revitalized, with all of its many themes reproduced in large and clear format, together with a detailed commentary.

Then around 1915, Rudolf Steiner created the sketches for a fourth series of zodiac images. These are quite different to the earlier images, and were to be carved into a blue window on the southern side of the Great Hall of the Goetheanum. He entrusted this work to a Russian artist, Assja Turgenieff. These images can be seen today, in the windows of the second Goetheanum. The oval painting from Stuttgart was many metres in diameter, and being painted on the ceiling, it has no top or bottom; it can be viewed from any angle. The old 1947 Almanac which I bought in the second hand bookstore reports that the figures "were painted in a light yellow colour on a dark blue background", see Illustration 1. The images in this book were created by scanning into a computer the four black and white photos, taken in approximately 1913. Once the difficulty of enhancing the texture of the photos (the 'dpi' count) was completed, to allow them to be printed as a large size poster, the colours were then carefully added, although I cannot know how precisely these colours correspond to those in the original painting.

1 The 1912 Stuttgart zodiac (re-created from black/white photos)

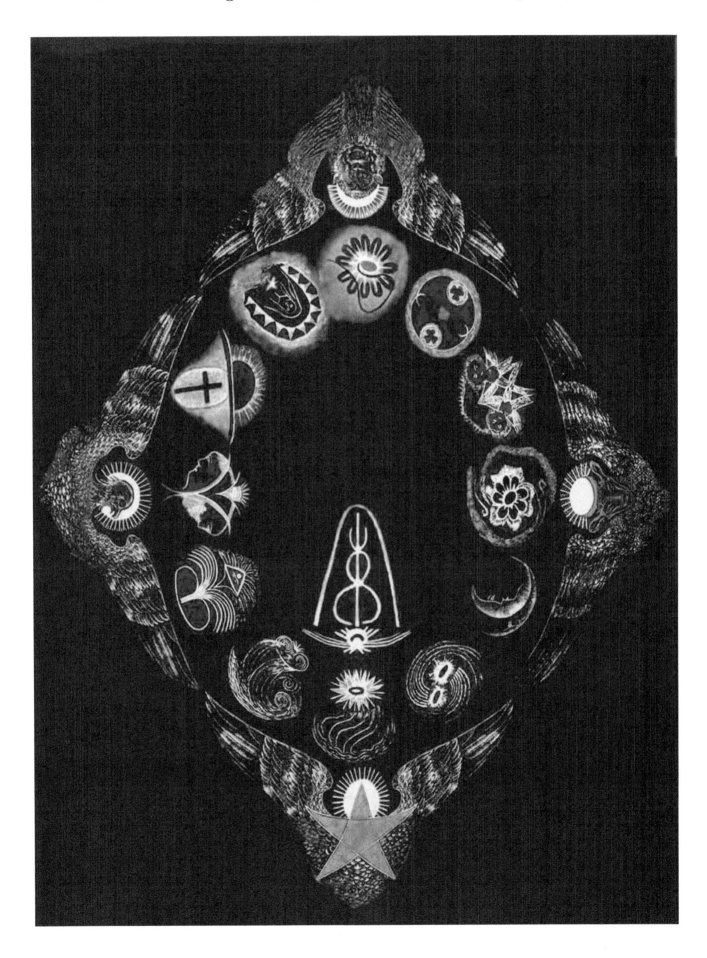

Chapter 1   The meaning of the twelve images in the Stuttgart zodiac painting

Overview

This zodiac painting has a thirteenth image, which is not a zodiac figure; it has some resemblance to the Staff of Hermes (also called the Caduceus) and it seems to relate to the future goal of the anthroposophical movement. We shall contemplate it later in this chapter. Forming a kind of periphery around the entire zodiac are four images, four winged entities. These are a version of the four famous apocalyptic creatures mentioned in the Book of Ezekiel and in the Book of Revelation. Traditionally, these are a lion, a bull, an eagle and a human being, and they represent the zodiac energies from Leo, Taurus, Scorpio and Aquarius, respectively. These are the four major zodiac forces, as each was the key zodiac source of the creative powers flowing from the spiritual worlds, during the four aeons, or vast evolutionary periods, known as the Saturn, Sun, Moon and Earth aeons; see illustrations 2,3,4 and 5. It is interesting to note that Scorpio is represented here by an eagle, not a scorpion; in this feature, we can see that Rudolf Steiner is affirming that Scorpio can also be symbolised by an eagle.

But despite the correlation of these four creatures to the four aeons, three of these four winged entities appear to refer to actual species of animals of today, rather than to the remote evolutionary stages of the Earth's history. For here these classical figures have undergone a profound metamorphosis. Firstly, the human being or Angel has been replaced with a winged star, which has a sun-like figure at its head. The bull figure is not a heavy, solid bull, but rather it is elegant, with almost a delicate deer-like quality. Similarly, the lion figure has a gentle, pleasant, warm-hearted quality, not a ferocious quality; and the eagle is not a formidable bird with a sharp beak and piercing eyes, but unthreatening. In contemplating these figures, I have the impression that three of these images represent the group-spirit of the relevant species. Rudolf Steiner taught that these group-spirits, living in the astral realm, are very wise beings and more noble in their nature and appearance than their creatures living down in the physical world.[1]

The Aquarian figure, which is usually an Angel, in Biblical art, is here a five-pointed star or pentagram. This star represents the Spirit-self in anthroposophy, hence so we can conclude this fourth figure refers to the Spirit-self or higher aspect of the human being. The Angel in the traditional versions also would seem to refer to the higher aspect of the human being, rather than the earthly person.

The background to the Stuttgart zodiac
We need to note that this zodiac depicts the interaction between humanity and the divine-spiritual beings active in the zodiac, in their work of creating and evolving humanity, over long ages. Some of the images refer back to past cycles of time, but some of the images refer to our future.

We shall start our exploration at the end of the zodiac cycle, with the image for Pisces. The reason for adopting this sequence is that all these images allude to the evolutionary

---

[1] For example in lectures on the Gospel of St. John, (GA 112), lect. 1st July 1909, and lects. 7th June 1908 & 1st Dec. 1907 (GA 98).

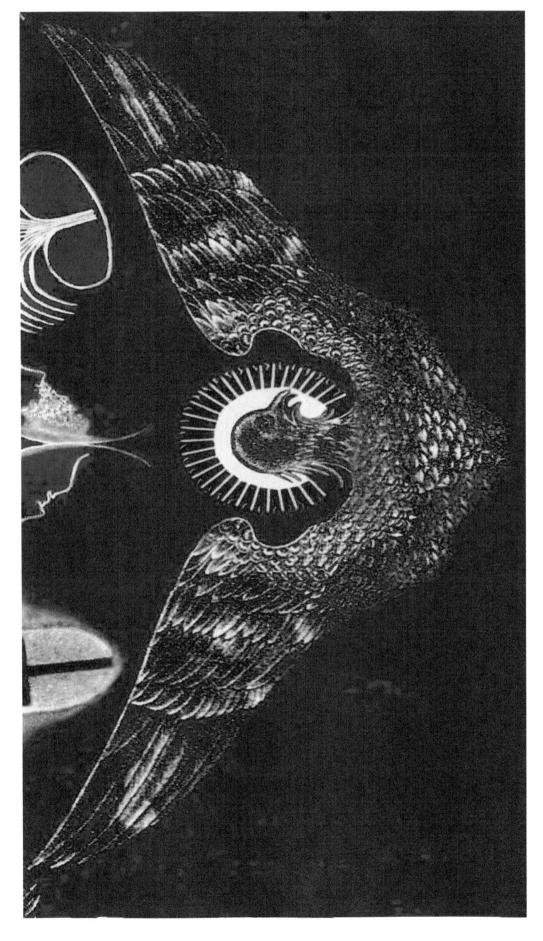

2   The Scorpio Eagle in the Stuttgart zodiac

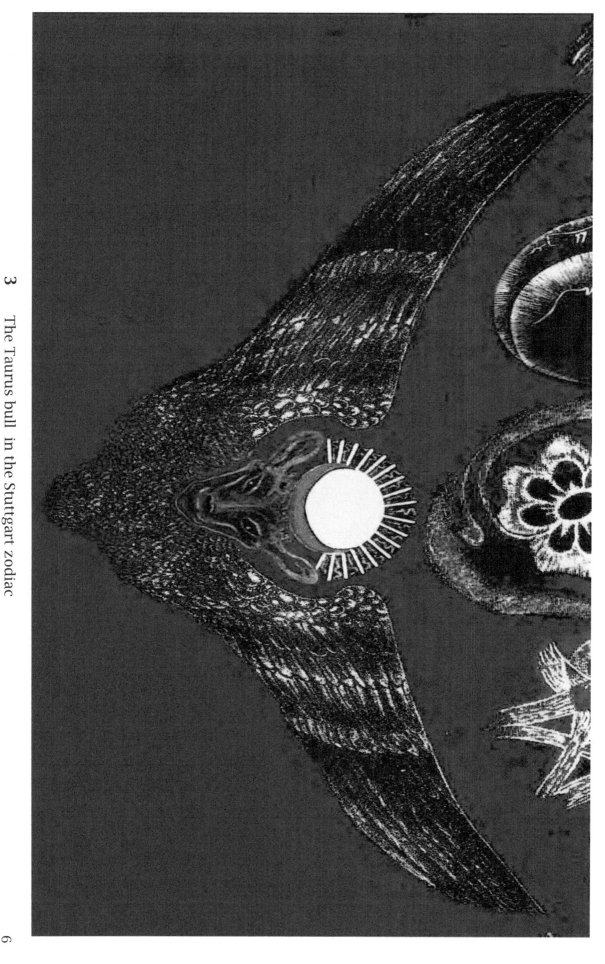

The Taurus bull in the Stuttgart zodiac

4   The Aquarius star in the Stuttgart zodiac

journey of the human life-wave, but the sequence starts in the past, with the Polarian large epoch, which was when the Pisces phase occurred.

After this epoch came the Hyperborean large epoch, and then the Lemurian epoch, which ended about 24,000 BC. See Illustration 6 for an overview of that section of the evolutionary journey of humanity which relates to these twelve images.[2] The old Polarian large epoch then, lies far back in time, and was itself a recapitulation of the much more remote Saturn Aeon. The ancient Piscean phase is correlated to Polaria, but also extending over into early Hyperborea. Rudolf Steiner describes the Earth in the Polarian epoch as a "fire-oval", but we need to note that this primarily ethereal 'planet', was still existing, as an identifiable area, within the sun. It was a definable area within the primordial sun, and would be cast out of it in the next Age, the Hyperborean Age.

The ancient Pisces phase: what we went through then
Near the surface of the pre-Earth planetary mass in Polaria there were ethereal egg-shaped oval forms, which also had a tenuous physical presence, composed of streams of warmth, see Illustration 7. The oval-shaped physical-etheric 'humans' were more present over the polar regions of the planet than other areas. Rudolf Steiner describes human beings of that Age as 'incarnating' into the "fire-mist"; he calls these human beings "sons of the fire-mist" (*Feuernebel* in German).[3] But human beings in Polaria also had an astral body, or soul, which existed somewhat higher up, in what we could call today our atmosphere, but this primordial soul was enveloped in the Angel who looks after each human being.

In this Age the pre-Earth planet, still inside the sun, developed a very tenuous, warm, gaseous element. This primordial Earth, with its delicate physical gaseous materials condensed over millions of years. This densification process, which would continue to affect the Earth, resulted in a vaporous, watery quality developing. This new stage led to the Earth being cast out of the sun, or as Rudolf Steiner taught, describing it from the viewpoint of humanity, in *An Outline of Esoteric Science*, the mighty sun withdrew from the Earth. This is the beginning of the Hyperborean Age. Our planet then became a satellite of the sun, and over millions of years, the planet continued to become more dense. On this highly ethereal, very warm, gaseous and now slightly watery planet, a multitude of partly ethereal, partly physical marine life began to appear. For this reason, the ancient initiates of Sumeria, where astrology began, designated this epoch by an image of fish. This idea was taken up and transmitted on into the time of the Roman Empire, where the name, Pisces, was given to it; a word which in Latin means 'fishes'.

The zodiac image painted in Stuttgart for the Pisces Age shows two dark ovals, each with a radiant glow around them, and trailing a kind of multi-stream curved tail (see Illustration 7). We can conclude that these two oval shapes, with their swirls of energy, represent two human beings, in terms of their physical-etheric body, which developed back in the Polarian epoch, but depicted in the early Hyperborean epoch. This conclusion is confirmed by Rudolf Steiner's own words about the Polarian epoch and this zodiac.[4] However, the choice by the initiate Rudolf Steiner to show *two* such forms, enables this new image to correlate to the traditional symbol for Pisces in astrology since ancient Sumerian time, namely that of two fishes. But in this way, it also alludes to our two feet, and our feet are governed by Piscean forces.

What does all of this have to with a Piscean person? The deep spiritual message in the Stuttgart zodiac is that **the dynamics which humanity underwent from Pisces, in a past Age, reflect in the psychology and often in the physiology of the people today who are born under that**

----

[2] For a clear diagram of the over-all evolutionary time-cycles through which humanity has passed, and shall pass in the future, see my *Rudolf Steiner Handbook*.

[3] From an archive document of July 1904.

[4] This is in an article from Feb. 1905, in the magazine "Lucifer-Gnosis".

5   The Leo lion in the Stuttgart zodiac

zodiac sign. Physiologically, we can note that from this simple oval form, the entire body later developed; so it is as if the rest of the body evolved up from the feet. These elliptical warmth-ovals of that remote Age, from which the rest of the body developed, have their after-echo today in the soles of our feet. From this evolutionary process, the therapeutic system known as 'zone-therapy' has its validity. It accurately stipulates that all the different organs and parts of the body are located in a zone somewhere on the soles of the feet. As I noted in the *Horoscope Handbook*, it is interesting that there is a fish species called *sole*, and when bunions form on our feet they are called 'fish-eyes'. This usage of words seems to indicate a veiled awareness, deep in the subconscious, of a common Piscean link between our feet and marine life. The validity of zone-therapy was acknowledged by Rudolf Steiner when he advised a student who was confined to a wheel-chair, because of extreme pain in her feet, to ignore her feet and use an anthroposophical medicament for her spleen. As this medicine was used, and the abdominal organ healed, the pain in her feet went away. No doubt the pain came from the spleen 'zone' of the sole.[5]

Furthermore, the primary feature of Piscean people is that quality of being sensitive and non-demanding, and of giving way to a higher authority or a noble ideal. The Piscean will surrender his or her own wants and rights if asked, or even if this is just an unspoken need with someone else. So a selflessness or humility is often a feature of the Piscean. Our feet are our interface with the ground, and this humble role enables the entire body to be upright and to move around. Also, the largest skin pores are in the soles; these large pores release into the soil (or our socks) the toxins which drain down to the feet. The Piscean is sensitive, often psychic, and generally has an acute capacity to feel what is going on in other people. Likewise our feet are especially tender, and sensitive to the touch. In the Piscean person, there is also a tendency to melt away into a larger reality, to dissolve the own ego's wants and drives, if this can give them a place in a larger, enveloping, inspiring milieu or group of people.

In the area of mysticism, of seeking spiritual experiences, the evolved Piscean has a natural ability to attain a consciousness which is one with the Divine. (But in negative situations, this means being attracted to unwholesome, consciousness-weakening mental exercises, through various kinds of unsuitable meditation or psychic exercises.) Likewise, in the ancient Polarian epoch and on into early Hyperborea, the multitudes of human beings moved as an integral part of a larger, spiritual reality: this was the 'Adam Kadmon' of ancient esoteric wisdom, that is the Earth regarded as formed entirely of a primal human being. There was no sense of, nor impulse towards, becoming a separate entity. As Rudolf Steiner told one small close group, "....the Earth and humanity was then but a single large living being, if one looked at it spiritually. The human beings were separate entities, but their consciousness was a common unity."[6]

Rudolf Steiner reports that the primordial rudimentary soul then had a kind of etheric hearing; this was a sense by which we could move through the etheric environment. This hearing was more a sense of inner touching. The Piscean today has an enhanced capacity for 'inner hearing', through which they know what other people want. This is also a kind of subtle sensing of their environment.

A note about the time-cycle involved
When the term 'the Piscean Age' is used or 'the Aquarian Age' and so on, this is actually a simplification. There was never a long age wherein the sun was only in a particular sector of the zodiac for long ages. Actually, the sun would shine down on to the ancient Earth from all of the zodiac groupings many times, in sequence as it moved through the entire zodiac. But what developed in each of these so-called Ages, developed evermore as the sun returned to that particular zodiac sector. So each time the sun entered Pisces during the Hyperborean phase, it

---

[5] The lady was Julie Klima, who recorded this in her memoirs.
[6] From an archive document of Berlin, April 1904; notes by F. Seiler.

Polaria	Hyperborea	late Hyperborea	early Lemuria	mid-Lemuria
Gen 1:1 The Elohim created Heaven & Earth. Ethereal pre-humans in the polar regions of pre-Earth globe	Sun leaves Earth; the Kant-Laplace nebula arises in space. The Earth develops a watery-vaporous element	Earth condenses ever more; many aquatic life-forms now appear	Earth, turbulent & volcanic, now has fluidic mineral substances.	The moon leaves the Earth, 18 million years ago
PISCES	**PISCES - AQUARIUS**	**CAPRICORN**	**CAPRICORN -SAGITTARIUS**	

Mid-Lemuria	late Lemuria	Atlantean	Post-Atlantean	'Manichaean'	(unnamed)
As the Earth settles down, souls return & humanity splits into 2 sexes	Luciferic beings stimulate individualized desires & thoughts	The "actual human epoch" during which the soul is enabled to develop spirituality	The "actual human epoch" during which the soul is to continue to develop spirituality	Half-way through the 6th Large Epoch this Virgo time ends, ca. 16,000 AD	
SCORPIO	**LIBRA**	**VIRGO**	**VIRGO**	**VIRGO**	**LEO ~ CANCER**

The 7 cultural epochs in the large Post-Atlantean Epoch indicated above: we are now in the 5th epoch

UrIndian   Urpersian   Egypto-Mesopotam   Greco-Latin   Anglo-European   Slavic   North American

11

Two tenuous rudimentary oval shaped bodies of humanity in the Polarian Epoch, mainly consisting of streams of warmth.

was the Piscean energy that was especially enhanced. We shall refer to all these repeated times of exposure to a zodiac sector in the evolutionary process, as a "phase"; thus *the Sagittarian phase*, etc.

The ancient Aquarian phase: what we went through then

The Aquarian image from Stuttgart shows an oval-shaped form with a radiant starry aura, hovering above a watery world, and connected by lines of energy, see illustration 8. The ancient evolutionary Aquarian phase first occurred during mid-Hyperborea (see illustration 6). So the influence of Aquarian energies on humanity was enhanced each time the sun entered the Aquarian sector of the zodiac during that time. The human being, in its attempts to be incorporated into an earthly body, now had to struggle to be in a body that had an increasingly dense, watery nature, although it was by our standards a delicate ethereal, gaseous watery organism. For this body continually dissolved and re-formed itself; in this process the human being was trying to establish its own boundaries or periphery within its misty, warm, watery environment.[7] Rudolf Steiner describes the human being's body in early Hyperborea, as appearing like a somewhat ethereal aquatic plant. But gradually the lower part of the body – from the ankles down – took on a somewhat fish-like appearance, and in the watery depths, murky aquatic creatures appear, some only ethereal, others having a tenuous physical body.

Physiologically, the Aquarian forces govern the ankles, and Rudolf Steiner describes how the primordial human being made effort to become 'incarnate' as it were, into the physical-etheric body, in the increasingly dense earthly environment. He describes the situation as "being 'incarnate' in a body in the air", but in "air which was thicker than today's atmosphere….with a oscillating motion, continuously vibrating through and through."[8] This body had a delicate flower-like shape, and it hovered precariously above the turbulent watery world, dissolving in the day-time phases and re-forming itself in the night-time phases. In this mid-period of Hyperborea, human beings used what we now have as ankles to steer themselves through their watery environment. And it was this submerged part of the body which gradually became more dense.

Psychologically, the Aquarian person of today echoes the dynamics of that ancient time through his or her inherent urge to get away from restrictions, and also through the struggle to establish boundaries. Though they don't want to actually merge right into a group, they do have a strong urge to be part of an always changing, stimulating environment of many friends, yet always maintaining their own independent ways of thinking and being. The human being was affected by tones from divine creative beings, resonating from the tone-ether and through the watery environment, moulding the physical-etheric body.

As I explained in *The Horoscope Handbook*, as an after-echo of our existence in this ancient resonating ethereal environment, evolved Aquarians often have a capacity for insights or intuitive flashes, which show that they are sensitive to ideas moving through the ether. In the next chapter we shall see the pencil drawing for Aquarius published in the 1912/13 Calendar, which displays this dynamic in a different way. We shall also come back to this theme when we explore the meditation verse for Aquarius from Rudolf Steiner, given in the *Twelve Moods*.

---

[7] Ref 5: archive document of July 1904.
[8] In Egyptian Myths, GA 106, lecture 7.

The human being striving to retain its tenuous airy-watery bodily form within the restlessly surging waves of the Earth in the Hyperborean Epoch.

The human being, with elemental energies, striving to maintain its hold on the increasingly dense body, during the late Hyperborean Epoch.

The ancient Capricorn phase: what we went through then

The image for the ancient Capricorn phase is very striking, see Illustration 9. We shall explore more about the reason for this strange image when we consider the variations depicted in the Calendar of 1912/13. This phase commenced in late Hyperborea, and continued into early Lemuria. It was in this period of time that the fluidic globe began to enter its 'earth' condition, that is, the watery element condensed and mineral substances, though still in a gaseous or fluidic state, began to appear. This will be one reason for Capricorn being regarded as an earth sign in astrology.

The ahrimanic forces start to manifest now, and in this still mainly aquatic environment of primordial oceans with some slightly more solid masses, the dragon-like or reptilian aquatic creatures began to appear. The human being, which has until now had a more delicate plant-like aquatic body, with a somewhat angelic ether form hovering above, transformed into an ugly, somewhat serpentine, fish form. As we shall see in the next chapter, this is the phase when the ahrimanic Double of the human being was formed.

This phase Rudolf Steiner describes as the 'wintertime' of the Earth, as the planet became increasingly dense, and a sinister influence arose from ahrimanic beings, who helped form the dense, deadened mineral substances. Less and less of the primitive human beings of that time could 'incarnate' into these denser bodies. Only those human beings with a higher capacity to push on and endure such difficult circumstances could find a foothold on the Earth. Now, the figure in the Stuttgart zodiac portrays what Rudolf Steiner described to Imma von Eckhardtstein as 'faun-like', which in effect means a denizen of the realm of faery, but not a particularly noble type of entity.

And yet this graphic is also about the human being in the Age of Capricorn, who, in striving to incarnate, is interacting with the denser aquatic and material environment. For us today, the idea of incarnating into a protoplasm body is quite normal; but before the primordial Age of Capricorn human beings were never required to penetrate with their astral nature into mineralized, deadened matter.

This challenge was there, even though the physical body was much less solid than ours, and also separated itself into segments as well as at times partially dissolving away and then re-forming (as indicated in the 1012/13 Calendar graphics). In contemplating this faun figure, I have the impression that it points towards the more dense, gnome-like elemental forces, and hence to somewhat ahrimanized etheric-astral (elemental) energies becoming assimilated into humanity in this Age. As we noted above, the more dense part of the physical body of the human being in this Age, submerged within the primordial ocean, degraded into an ugly fish-serpent form. It is also worth noting that the symbol of this sign, going back into Babylonian times (and no doubt into earlier Sumerian times) is not actually that of a mountain goat, it is an entirely mythical creature, a goat-fish.

These dynamics are reflected in the psychology of people today who are born as Capricorns. People born in this sign have the strongest capacity of the entire zodiac signs to persevere, to endure hardship and continue on with their goal. Moreover, they also can manifest the greatest capacity to decide upon a goal which may lie decades ahead, and yet persevere through all obstacles, until they reach their goal. In the next chapter we shall consider the anti-social, ego-centric side of the Capricorn double. It is clear, from Rudolf Steiner's description of the evolution of humanity in these earlier Ages, guided by divine beings, that the intention was clearly there, with the hierarchical beings, for human beings to eventually become people in a flesh and blood body living in many incarnations on a solid Earth. And this intention was reflected in the intentions of humanity, raying in from each person's guiding Angel, to strive for incarnation, and to push on with this effort, so that the experience of being incarnate in a sophisticated and stable body could be a reality by the time of the Atlantean Age.

The ancient Sagittarian phase: what we went through then
As the early phase of Lemuria progressed, we came into the Sagittarian Age. On the Stuttgart ceiling, the image for humanity in this age has a geometrical basis to it, see Illustration 10. There is the lower oval, with two sides, and rising up from this are six energy lines, raying out left and right. Above this is a stylised image of a face in a triangle, above this is a kind of aura, and below a somewhat triangular shape suggests energies pushing down into the turbulent space below. This phase takes us from fairly early Lemuria up to mid-Lemuria. What kind of experiences did we go through then? Human beings were then aquatic creatures, in an increasingly dense world, having what Rudolf Steiner described as "cold, white blood, and it is this factor which made it possible for humanity to exist in a watery environment".[9]

By now islands and larger areas of more dense material, of soil and rocks, were forming out of the water, and warmer semi-solid areas gave rise to volcanic eruptions frequently. In this world, human beings, along with various forms of marine life, began to evolve lungs, to make it possible to live out of the water, on the still turbulent landmasses. It is fascinating to learn that, because of the inherent link of the human life-wave to the whole Earth, this very substantial metamorphosis in humanity's physiology resulted in the coming into being of birds.

To see why this is the case, we just need to recall what we noted earlier. It was in the Polarian Age that the 'Adam Kadmon' situation prevailed. That is, the entire globe was an undifferentiated unified organism; a kind of global human soul. The Earth was created primarily so that we humans could eventually emerge, and as we evolved the animals came into existence as separate life-waves, embodying the astrality cast-off from us.[10] So all of that we now have as animals all around us, was then part of the Earth's astral aura. This Sagittarian Age, in which bird-species appeared, correlates to what is called the Triassic Age in geology. Although in the anthroposophical worldview, this epoch occurs much more recently than in geological understanding; for more about this see my *Rudolf Steiner Handbook.*

The Stuttgart graphics for Sagittarius direct our attention to the great effort that human beings made in the first half of the Lemurian Age to incarnate. Also there is a face implied in the image, indicating that a more recognizably human being now exists. It is the task of the soul to try to penetrate into this much more solid physical world; hence the 'gesture' of the image here is like an arrow moving downwards, reminiscent of the traditional symbol for Sagittarius. Rudolf Steiner referred to these as "raying-in light" streaming into a "water-air" atmosphere.[11] But this image, with its energy lines, raying out left and right, also alludes to that turbulent, highly volcanic environment in which silica and other minerals were, in Rudolf Steiner's words, 'raining down' through the watery atmosphere.

This precipitation began to gradually form the planet's core. We can note here that these twice six lines of energy, raying out left and right, depict twelve lines of energy, the zodiac number. Rudolf Steiner taught that cosmic music or spiritual energies raying in from the divine beings active in the zodiac, resonating through the ethers, especially in the water-ether (or tone-ether), were creating the many beautiful geometrical shapes which we now see in the solid rocks and gems around us. They gained these patterns and shapes from the motion of the twelve-fold zodiacal energies, whose patterns, pulsing through the primeval Earth, were frozen into permanency as the Earth hardened. Rudolf Steiner refers to this as the primordial 'dance of matter' in response to the music of the heavens. The above dynamics of the Sagittarian phase

---

[9] Ref. 7: archive document from July 1904.
[10] For more about the casting-off of minerals, plants and animal species. see my *Two Gems from Rudolf Steiner.*
[11] Rudolf Steiner to Imma von Eckhardtstein, in the Beiträge zur GA, Nr. 37-38 p. 83.

The human soul striving to enter into an increasingly dense bodily form within the solidifying but still volatile, volcanic Earth in the early Lemurian Epoch.

are echoed in the Sagittarian person of today. For people whose sun-sign (or rising sign) is in Sagittarius, are especially drawn to exerting their will out into the world. This urge does echo the ancient dynamic the Sagittarian Age, of penetrating the world with one's will. But in particular, the Sagittarian is drawn to any initiative which gives an opportunity to respond to grand ideas. That is, ideas which challenge the person to go beyond their normal horizons and attitudes; these are especially appealing. When we explore the Sagittarius graphic depicted from the 1912/13 Calendar, the meaning of the Stuttgart image will become clearer.

The ancient Scorpio phase: what we went through then
Towards the end of the Sagittarian epoch, which correlates to the end of what in geology is called the Permian epoch, the planet became ever more hardened, and, to preserve its capacity as a habitation for humanity, the moon was cast out. This occurred some 18 million years ago, and caused enormous catastrophes to the still pliable, fiery volcanic world. Only a tiny number of human beings survived this event. Human beings began to return into bodies that now developed cartilage. Previously they were composed mainly of soft gelatinous material. Within a relatively short time, a very major change occurred: humanity spilt into the two sexes, so the older hermaphrodite condition was ending. Mars forces permeated the planet and red-blood began to course through the veins. With only half the etheric forces available to the human being now for reproduction, both sexes were required. But this change allowed the gradual formation of the brain, at least in a rudimentary form.

Bearing in mind what we have noted above, the Stuttgart graphic for the Scorpio phase becomes quite clear. It shows humanity splitting into man and woman, and above is a radiant image, indicating the activity of the energies which were to commence the development of individual thinking, see Illustration 11. It was millions of years before the type of individualized consciousness arises that we have known ever since the Hellenistic Age; but it begins in a small way in this epoch, due to the influence of Scorpio. In this way, an inner life was actually to arise for human beings: that is, an intellectual capacity and also personal yearnings, feelings and sensual desires.

In this epoch too, Luciferic angels and archangels from Venus and Mercury begin to exert their influence in the thinking and emotions of primitive human beings. It is this dynamic which became known as the Fall of Man in theology, although it did start to a lesser degree, in the Lemurian period before the moon was cast out. The story of Eve tempting Adam with fruit from the Tree of Knowledge of Good and Evil refers to this. Rudolf Steiner explains that 'Eve' represents the sentient soul, that is, the emotions and desires within the human being. An additional dynamic here is that Ahrimanic powers gain a new impetus in the lower astral forces of human beings through this succumbing to Luciferic influences.

The Scorpio person today strongly echoes these dynamics which so facilitate separating human consciousness from higher beings, and yet also build the basis for individualization, and thus inner freedom. The Scorpio person has a particularly strong awareness of their inner life, as their thoughts, feelings and desires have an intensity that other zodiac signs rarely equal. Sexuality can consequently be a problem, and in addition, the intensity with which they experience their ideas leads them to refrain from manifesting this, because they doubt whether other people can perceive and really acknowledge this intensity.

The ancient Libra phase: what we went through then
The image for Libra depicts the horizon of the Earth, with the sun rising above it, and beneath the horizon line is a radiant area, inside of which is a brighter shield-shaped area with a cross in it; see Illustration 12. We know that the symbol for Libra in traditional astrology is an outline of a set of scales or balances. To understand the striking image from Stuttgart, we need to recall that zodiac energies are called 'ascending' and 'descending' by Rudolf Steiner. He taught that

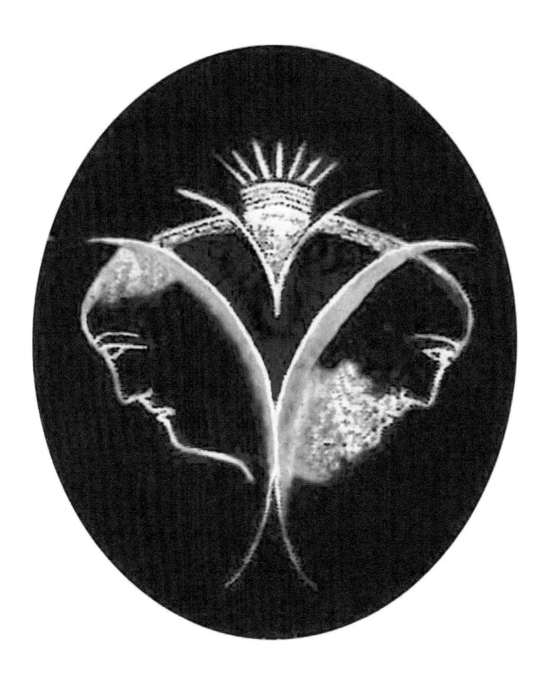

In mid-Lemuria as human beings returned to populate the Earth, after the moon was cast out, the two sexes developed, releasing etheric energy for the development of the brain, as the instrument of thinking.

During the Libran phase of our evolution, there was balance or equilibrium in the cosmos between the 'ascending' and the 'descending' zodiac influences. Now the ego-sense in human beings began to emerge, a pointer to the future Mystery of Golgotha.

there are seven 'ascending' forces and five 'descending' ones. These terms refer to the descent of guiding spiritual energies from the zodiac to the Earth, and that, once this process has ennobled humanity, then humanity sends back to the heavens as it were, qualities of the soul, such as thoughts, higher emotions and will. Once this happens that zodiac sign is no longer a 'descending' one, but an ascending sign.

The **7** ascending signs are :
Aries   Taurus   Gemini   Cancer   Leo   Virgo   Libra
It is obvious that these energies have ennobled that zone of the body which they influence, bringing about the more noble upper part of the body.

The **5** descending signs are :
Scorpio Sagittarius Capricorn Aquarius Pisces
It is obvious that these energies have not as yet ennobled that zone of the body which they influence, and which remains in an inferior state to that of the upper body.

However, back in the Libran phase, which went from late Lemuria on into mid-Atlantis, this was not the situation. In late Lemuria, humanity was consolidating its capacity to walk fully upright, a process that requires the integration of the function carried out by the hips. However, the ability we humans have to remain upright is something that separates us from the animals. It is not our feet or hips that as such keep us upright, it is the ego which, in using these organs, strives for our vertical position. If we become faint, or lose consciousness, or go to sleep, we fall over, whereas quadruped animals, who live primarily in the horizontal position, can stay in horizontal even whilst asleep. So as the Libran phase began, Libran forces were *commencing* their task. This was not completed until the end of that phase of evolution, until then they were still 'descending' forces.

So during the Libran phase of our evolution, as regards humanity, there were six descending influences and six ascending influences.

The 6 ascending signs were :
Aries   Taurus   Gemini   Cancer   Leo   Virgo

The 6 descending signs were :
Scorpio Sagittarius Capricorn Aquarius Pisces Libra

So there was **a balance in regard to the cosmic forces operative at this time upon humanity;** six zodiac forces were ascending, six were descending. Rudolf Steiner taught that this cosmic balance condition is the reason for the ancient initiates devising the symbol of scales or a weighing balance for Libra. The Stuttgart graphic, in its upper outline, does actually incorporate the main design of the traditional symbol for Libra: that of a set of scales.

As this Libran epoch was ending, midway through the Atlantean Age, about 15,000 BC, spiritual forces became active to bring about a stronger ego-sense in human beings. From the sun-sphere, the cosmic Christ and other of the Spirits of Form (or Exousiai) rayed their influences into humanity. This process was undertaken to ensure that the ego-sense, as it consolidated itself in humanity, would retain an inherent connection to the Spiritual-Self (and also the Life-spirit and Spirit-human). In the next chapter we shall consider further this aspect of the Libran phase.

Librans today echo this dynamic, for they have a distinct struggle with their ego, their sense of self. They find it difficult to assert their ideas or attend to their own interests, for they have to struggle to find the balance between defending and affirming their own self, against the self of other people. That is, the Libran person has to struggle to affirm his or her values, or implement an intention, when someone else asserts their own will. Consequently the person

This image refers to the spiritualized, living cosmos which is experienced when the Spirit-self (or 'Sophia' quality) is developed in the soul.

with Libra as their sun-sign or rising sign is often beset with indecisiveness. There is deep-seated anxiety about disturbing the balance or status quo in social interactions; but there is also a gift at maintaining harmony in other aspects of life.

The Virgo phase: what we are going through now

The symbol for the Virgo phase in the Stuttgart ceiling is quite striking; and quite different from the graphic designed for the 1912/13 Calendar, which we shall consider in the next chapter. In this painting, we see a cloud-like surrounding, inside of which is a simple outline of a feminine figure; see Illustration 13. She does have similarities to depictions of the Virgin Mary, but also she actually has a cosmic quality, for around her is a radiant aura, but raying out in twelve areas. This figure is holding what appears to be either a dove, or a sun-like object. The entire image also merges slightly into the next image, that of Leo. In the zodiac constellations, the stars of Leo and of Virgo do slightly overlap.

So what stage of humanity's evolution does this image refer to? The artist Imma von Eckhardtstein, noted that she was told it "represents the entire epoch of humanity". What Rudolf Steiner means here is that it refers to that phase in which humanity could be said to exist as human beings, in terms of how we naturally define ourselves as people. Now, the question is, where is this phase, in terms of the flow of time? The Libran phase extended from late Lemuria on into mid-Atlantis, by which time human beings became what we would today refer to as human. So the Virgo phase commences as from mid-Atlantean times. But when does this Virgo phase end? On rare occasions Rudolf Steiner spoke of the daunting theme of the future, and what will happen to humanity in future time-cycles, in general terms.

From these indications, we learn that in the middle of the Manichaean large epoch,[12] (the epoch which succeeds our current Post-Atlantean epoch), most human beings shall cease to reincarnate, see Illustration 6.[13] But Rudolf Steiner also once indicated that the future Cancerian phase (see below) shall occur in the Manichaean large epoch. So we can reasonably conclude that the Virgoan phase, as meant in these zodiac graphics, starts about 15,000 BC and probably ends about AD 8000, when the Post-Atlantean Large Epoch ends. We note here that this Virgo phase is much shorter than the preceding epochs, all of which lasted millions of years. It is also quite possible that the later future phases are also of short duration, (We should note here also that before the late Hyperborean time the Earth was not yet cast of the sun, hence 'years' as we know them, did not exist.)

So what is being developed in humanity during this epoch? What does Virgo represent? The name of the constellation Virgo means in Latin, 'pure maiden', in India it is known as 'Kanya', i.e., virgin; and in Chinese it is 'She Sung Nu' which means 'purified maiden'. Whenever spiritual or esoteric traditions depict a venerable feminine figure, it represents spirituality, which we know as the Spirit-self (or Spiritual-self) in anthroposophy. From the earlier evolutionary phases humanity has gained an independent soul, and a sense of self. The task of the divine beings now, is to exert their efficacy from Virgo, so as to assist the astral body to transform, to some degree, into the Spirit-self. This means in effect, to overcome the lower, animal astral tendencies, from which we have been separating ourselves ever since the primeval ages of Hyperborea and Lemuria.

The Spiritual-self state of consciousness is indicated in the image by the surrounding radiant zodiacal glow. This feature indicates that humanity's consciousness is now starting once again to perceive the spiritual, and this imbues the cosmos with a supernal radiance. This state of consciousness, the clairvoyant, enlightened Spiritual-self is the same as what the ancients called the Isis or Sophia state. Much confusion occurs in anthroposophical literature about this word.

---

[12] I use this name for this epoch because a student of Rudolf Steiner reports that he stated that the high initiate Manes (or Mani) will be a significant spiritual leader in that epoch; (in lecture notes by Kurt Walther, undated).
[13] From an unpublished archive document of Oct. 1904.

It is incorrectly described as a goddess; religious sentiments lingering on from olden times have played a role in creating this error. In the 16 times in 354 volumes that Rudolf Steiner refers to these words, he defines the word Isis or Sophia, with only one exception, as the Spiritual-self, not as a goddess; "Isis is that being which in us goes from one life to the other".[14] A lack of clarity about this theme easily brings in an old religious nuance here, as a study of anthroposophy reveals. For example, Rudolf Steiner taught in regard to this theme that, "Mary, who gave birth to Jesus, had developed the Spirit-self, and **for this reason she was called "Sophia" by the early Christians**".[15] (Emphasis mine) So there was no goddess reposing in the aura of the Virgin Mary, but rather, 'Sophia' means that she had acquired the stage of Spirit-self.

Rudolf Steiner further explains the reason that the Greeks chose a feminine term, Sophia, is that "the earlier initiates noticed how cosmic energies streamed into the pure newly formed Spirit-self, (a feminine dynamic}...and hence they gave a feminine name to this fifth part of the human being ....".[16] In other words, with the clairvoyance of the Spiritual-self state, the acolyte felt his or her soul receiving the in-raying energies of the cosmos, and this kind of receiving is a feminine dynamic. The main occasion where Rudolf Steiner's words appear to refer to a goddess occurs in his famous lectures, *The Search for the Isis-Sophia*, which refer to the ancient Egyptian perspective. In this context, Rudolf Steiner explains that in Egypt, Isis was a depicted at times as a personification of the cosmos, now alive to clairvoyant vision with its many divine beings, nature spirits and general astral-etheric forces;

> Isis is the personified All-wisdom of *our* world...in her true figure, Isis is permeating the entire cosmos...she is that which shines radiantly towards us in many auric colours from the cosmos...[17]

On page 40 the theme of Sophia is explored further. These dynamics underlying the current phase, the Virgo phase, which aims to uplift the earthly human soul to the Spiritual-self, are echoed in the people today who have Virgo as their sun-sign (or rising sign). These people have a natural tendency towards purity and being prudent. Whether this focuses on soul purity, or mainly on a conscious approach to hygiene and orderliness, depends on the evolvement of that soul. But either of these, or both of these, is a well-known feature of the Virgoan person.

****

A new series of Seven and Five
We noted earlier that there are now seven 'ascending' zodiac influences and five 'descending' influences. In the Stuttgart zodiac, this pattern is reversed in an unusual way. There are seven influences which began in the **past**; from Pisces through to Virgo. Most of these are entirely in the past, except for Virgo which continues on for some 6,000 years or so. Then there are five **future** influences, from Leo through to Aries. These five start in the mid-Manichaean large epoch and continue on from there, but it is not known for how long each of these phases will last. And as they deal with the attaining of future spiritual consciousness, there is only a little that can be said about them, but the images are potent meditative aids to try to feel our way ahead into the future stages of human evolution.

The Leo phase: what we may achieve then
In the Stuttgart ceiling, all the images after the one for Virgo refer to future phases of humanity's evolution. From what we noted above, the Leo phase and then the Cancer phase

---

[14] GA 144, lecture 5.
[15] GA 97 p.58.
[16] Lect. 28th Mar. 1907, in GA 55 p.230.
[17] Lect. 24th Dec. 1910, in GA 202 p.238.

occur during the Sixth Large Epoch, the Manichaean epoch. Rudolf Steiner mentioned that the Leo graphic concerns the development of the heart chakra and that the dark line running through it is a mirror image of the traditional symbol for Leo, see Illustration 14. So this graphic depicts the heart area, with its 12-petalled chakra. When this chakra is developed, it bestows the capacity to perceive the inner warmth or coldness of other beings, and of the elemental forces in minerals and plants. It also bestows perception of the mood or mindset of other people.

In this image, the dark line represents the dispersion of the old forces in the blood, namely the luciferic forces. Rudolf Steiner mentioned to the painter that this transformative purifying of the astral body, with its effect on the heart chakra, is "the outcome of the crucifixion". This no doubt refers to the crucifixion of Jesus Christ, and the vital transformative power this sacred event had on the Earth's aura. The emphasis is being placed here on the Crucifixion, rather than the Resurrection, because it was then that the blood ran forth from Jesus, and as Rudolf Steiner taught, esoterically informed Christians saw in the blood that came forth from the wounds of the Redeemer an expression of the Higher Ego. These people said, "Whoever makes this blood living in them arrives at a true clairvoyance".[18] That is, the lower, earth-bound ego forces in the human being's astrality are overcome by this deed and the spiritual forces of the Redeemer.

It is a reasonable conclusion that a Leo person of today, who is truly seeking spiritual development could work especially towards this condition. Physiologically, Leo governs the heart, and Leo people do have a warm-hearted inclusiveness, which helps make them socially successful. Their social awareness can be quite strong, and this may form a natural basis for developing the sensitive social awareness that the heart chakra brings.

The Cancer phase: what we may achieve then
The next image in the Stuttgart zodiac represents the inner spiritual structure and attainment of humanity in the Cancer phase of our future, see Illustration 15. The image would remain an enigma if Imma von Eckhardtstein had not noted down that she was told it represents "the development of the chakras, and that here a radiant 'forward spinal column' is forming, and the {current} spinal column disappears." So the perspective here is as if one were looking down on a human being from above, in a future age. One sees the fully developed chakras, forming in effect a column of radiant astral energy. But in addition there is now an etheric column, formed from the fully developed etheric chakras. This etheric column bridges across to the astral column. In his private esoteric lessons Rudolf Steiner explained that as this future state arises, people will be able to function with their ego-sense (of a higher kind) in spirit realms.[19] It is reported that Rudolf Steiner stated privately that it would be some 20,000 years before this would be more generally achieved. See the remarks about the Cancer graphic in the Calendar 1912/13 for more about this.

This forming of an enveloping etheric bridge, is approximately similar, in a purely human sense, to the characteristic of the Cancerian person of being able to "bridge the space" between themselves and other people, by sensing the feelings of others. It is also the case that they make a kind of enveloping psychic shell into which they retreat, if they are feeling unhappy, or are wanting to avoid confrontations.

---

[18] From a lecture of 6th May 1909, in GA 57.
[19] References to this are to be found in GA 147 (lect. 26th Aug. 1913) and also GA 266b p.119 and GA 267 p.444.

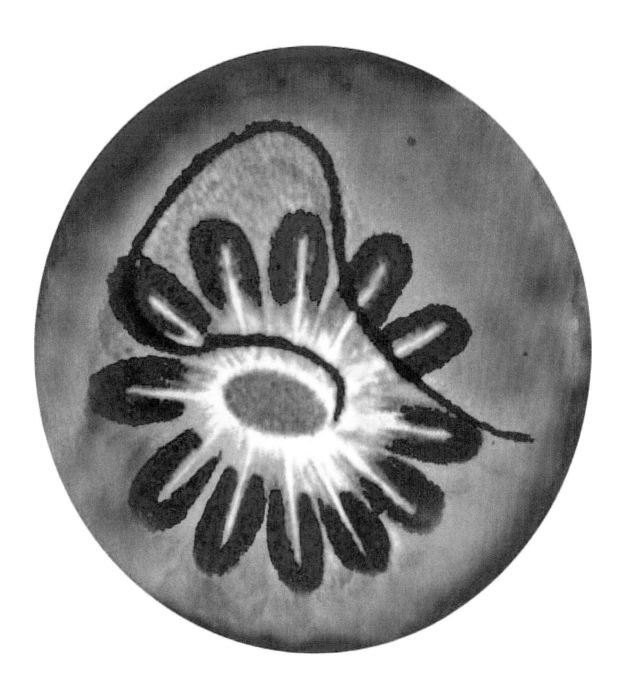

This Leo graphic refers to the future when the heart chakra is developed. This will be in the sixth Large Epoch.

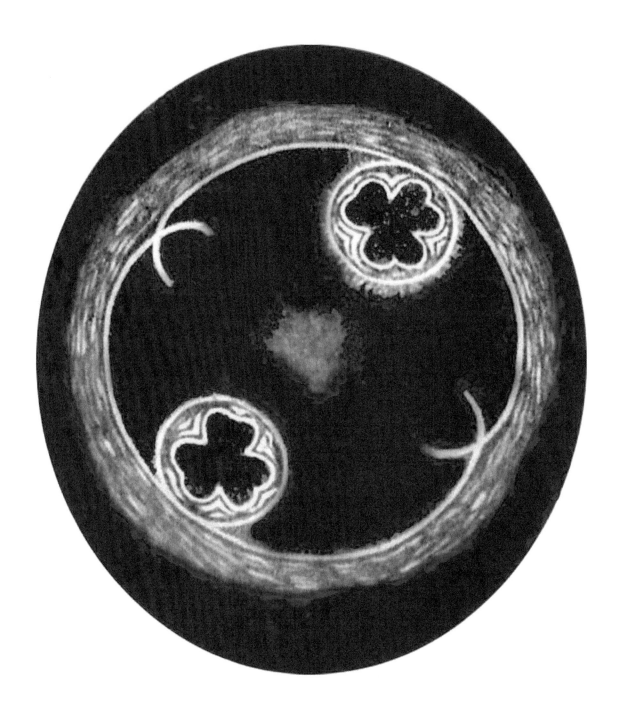

This graphic presents a view from above of the human being in the sixth Large Epoch, when in addition to the series of astral chakras, there is also a new column of etheric chakras which merge with these.

The future Gemini phase: what we may achieve then
The image for Gemini in the Stuttgart zodiac is a readily recognizable version of the traditional symbol. We see two children obviously feeling a bond to each other, in a kind of dance gesture, see Illustration 16. There exists very little in the way of information about this graphic artwork. Rudolf Steiner wrote in his sketch, for the similar image, published in the Calendar 1912/13, "small children, the physical weakness is mutually supported through spiritual strength".[20] We can feel that these children have both a star-like quality and a mood of rejoicing. There is also the nuance of the two people communing with each other, perhaps in a way that is beyond language, as we know it now.

Unfortunately, there are no indications as to what this future Gemini phase shall bring to humanity in the way of spiritual-psychological gifts. But it is well known that today Gemini people have a particular focus on conversing with people, they have a focus on speech; this often makes them talkative and outgoing. This tendency easily leads to an excessive sanguinity and superficiality, but not if the person is intent on meaningful communication. This image speaks of a unity between the two people, suggesting that the future Gemini phase will engender the capacity for inner unity with others, or spiritual community through having developed appropriate forms of sincere communicating.

The future Taurus phase: what we may achieve then
In the Stuttgart zodiac, the image for the Taurus phase is a flower-like form, with a delicate tracery-like aura, and enveloped in two outer swirls, see Illustration 17. There are eight petals to the flower-shape, so this image refers to the throat chakra which has 16 petals when fully developed; eight of these exist already. Although Taurus is closely associated with Venus, the throat chakra is a Mars-governed chakra; it is the additional eight petals or lines of force which need to be developed before it can become active. Once developed, it bestows the capacity to perceive thought-forms or ideas existing in the astral realm. In particular, it gives the capacity to perceive the thoughts of the gods which underlie creation.

A major soul quality which is needed for this chakra to become active is mildness of soul, or absence of that core negative Mars feature of aggression, especially harming others through one's words. This point about overcoming the negative Mars forces, is a teaching in that small anonymous booklet, *Light on the Path*; "Before the voice can speak in the presence of the Masters, it must have lost the power to wound." This indicates that noble Venus energies have triumphed over lower Mars forces. The artist noted a brief comment from Rudolf Steiner, "the larynx becomes creative in the word". In his notebook with the sketch for the 1912/13 Calendar, for Taurus, Rudolf Steiner wrote,

> "The voice, which did not {fully} fill the inner being of the soul, and thereby called forth real self-consciousness"[21]

Although this sentence is found on the same page of Rudolf Steiner's notebook which has a drawing for the Aries image, and the symbol of Aries, there is no evidence that it refers to Aries. For other pages of this notebook are also shared between sketches or words that refer to two zodiac signs; for example on the same page that has a sketch for Virgo, there is a sketch

---

[20] In the English edition of the 1912/13 Calendar, ed./trans. C. Bamford, the deciphering of these notes is not accurate; ("*small children who spiritually resemble ? each other*"). Comparison with Steiner's other notebook entries reveals that he wrote, '...phys. Schwäche...geistige Stärke..' (e.g., in Beiträge 106 & 108 & his handwritten corrections to the notes for a lecture in Oxford 19/Aug/1922.)
[21] In the English edition of the 1912/13 Calendar, ed. /trans. C. Bamford, the deciphering of these notes has an error,; ("*the voice that feels effort and thereby calls forth self-consciousness*"). Comparison with Steiner's other notebook hand-writing entries confirms that the unclear words are, 'nicht füllte'.

In this future phase, human beings become a kind of star-children, living in harmony with each other.

for Scorpio too, and this is the case for Leo and Gemini as well. I conclude that this sentence refers to the Taurus phase, not the phase of Aries. This sentence then refers to the power that the initiate gains, or human beings generally will have in the future, when this chakra is operative. Normally, planetary and zodiacal energies resonate in the vowels and consonants of language, but they are only in the background, the speaker is unaware of this. The sounds fill out the inner soul-awareness of the person as they speak, so he or she has no awareness of the cosmic origins of these sounds. These forces, underlying our speech, are in effect the cosmic Word, that is the expression in our soul of the influences of the zodiac and the planets. Also, Rudolf Steiner wrote on his sketch for a similar image, to be published in the Calendar 1912/13, "the voice which goes back in to the animal." This appears to refer to a negative dynamic about the voice; the opposite of an awakening to the cosmic forces behind speech.

For once that higher consciousness is attained which allows the human being to be master of his or her own etheric and astral forces, then these planetary and zodiacal energies will not be unconsciously spoken forth. The inner awareness of the soul will now cognize these forces and then they can be actively used, in a creative way; the "Lost Word" will be gradually be found. We need to note here that this Taurus phase is to occur in the future, when many people come to the last of their incarnations. So it is difficult to visualize the actual circumstances that will prevail when we human beings experience the throat-chakra in such a future state. According to a brief statement from Rudolf Steiner, this future Taurus phase will occur during the fourth Age (of 2,160 years) of the sixth Large Epoch, which we can call the Manichaean epoch.[22]

The future Aries phase: what we may achieve then
The ceiling in Stuttgart shows a very evocative image here for the Aries Age, being a masterly transformation of the traditional symbol of Aries, having two horns of a ram's head, see Illustration 18. The two horns here are now two interfaces of the human being with the world around them, thus showing two faces in profile. The outermost face is gazing at the sense world, whilst the inner face is gazing into a radiant spiritual realm.

This image is directing our contemplations to a spiritual perceiving (or seership) in addition to the normal sensory perception. Bearing in mind that it is about our consciousness in a distant epoch, we see that it is proclaiming a future time when we can see into spiritual realms as the normal state of consciousness. But this particular way of depicting such seership takes on a deeper meaning when we know that the Aries person of today has a natural capacity for 'inner seeing', so to speak. That is, she or he subtly perceives ideas, and then acts on them. The urge for activity, which is so strong with Aries people, starts with an idea, an idea which they usually have perceived more clearly in their mind's eye, than other people.

The forehead is the area governed by Aries, and it is here that we have an area of the brain through which we experience our thoughts. This kind of perceiving could be called a kind of veiled seership. But it is also here, on the etheric-astral level that the organ for clairvoyance, the so-called third eye, exists. This chakra has two streams of energy in it, referred to as two petals. So the Stuttgart ceiling image is merging the two horns of the ram with the two-petalled chakra, and depicting how through this people in the future become clairvoyant ! Now that we have explored the meaning of this image, we can better understand the indications made by Rudolf Steiner about it. Imma von Eckhardtstein notes that he commented to her:

> 1 "The human being {now} lives in fact still in the physical {realm} and {yet} at the same time a spiritual existence {the two profiles} – he gazes at Jupiter."

> 2 "The horns of Aries are the {two} optic nerves: one in the physical world, one in the spiritual world".

---

[22] From a lecture of 5th Nov. 1904, published in GA 89.

31

This graphic presents the soul a future Age when the throat chakra is developed in humanity.

Here the future phase of humanity is depicted when the Aries forces can be used for seership as distinct from the usual sensory perceiving.

Comment 1 is quite clear, it summarises what we have said above, plus it adds a reference to looking towards Jupiter, which presumably means the next aeon, implying that humanity in the Taurus phase shall have an awareness of this next aeon.

Comment 2 is fairly clear, it is presumably suggesting as a poetic picture, rather than a medical fact, that one of the optic nerves will serve for sense perception, the other for seership.[23]

The additional Caduceus image

The first feature of this unusual symbol is, **that it is placed next to the image for Aquarius**, that is, for the Aquarian phase of our past evolution, which took place as we saw earlier, in the Hyperborean time, see Illustration 19. But when contemplating this symbol, I had the impression that it does not refer back to that ancient Aquarian phase, but rather, forwards to the next cultural epoch, that is the Sixth Post-Atlantean epoch, which is also called the Age of Aquarius. This age commences in AD 3573 and lasts for 2,160 years. In the middle of this age will be the next time that the Sun archangel will influence humanity's cultural life. These archangelic phases of influencing the soul-life of human beings, last for about 350-380 years (so in the Sixth epoch, this will be from about AD 4400 to 4780).

In our times the Sun archangel is the great archangel Michael, as in earlier ages too, but in the 6th post-Atlantean epoch it shall be another archangel, for by then Michael shall have arisen to the hierarchical level of Principality. It is this segment of the future Aquarian Age that is intended to allow a golden age of cultural-spiritual blossoming to take place. Rudolf Steiner's lecture "*Preparing for the Sixth Epoch*" explains that one of the purposes of the coming into being of anthroposophy in our times is to help ensure that this blossoming does in fact happen. So, as the anthroposophists gathered in this building, often in the presence of Rudolf Steiner, this additional image reminded them of the great future mission which lay behind their spiritual work.

Now this symbol is in essence a Caduceus, or the 'staff of Hermes', which has various meanings in anthroposophy. The meaning which is relevant here, is that one where Rudolf Steiner explains that it represents our consciousness during the day-time and during the night-time. It speaks of how the process of spiritual development enables the meditant to gradually gain awareness of the night-time immersion in the spiritual realms and how to integrate the night-time and the day-time experiences.

But above this symbol, which is en-clothed in an arc, is what appears to be a metamorphosis of a winged sun-disk. That is, it is a sun-symbol, in which the moon is enclosed, and from which various rays of light stream out. This may represent the birth of the Spiritual-self from the advanced consciousness that integrates day and night experiences, in the more advanced souls of that future Age.

Another way to understand this additional image is to contemplate its companion symbol, in the Calendar of 1912/13. We shall be exploring these zodiac symbols in the next chapter. But here we can explore the associated Caduceus symbol from that book, see Illustration 20. This image was placed without any comment, next to the month of October. In terms of the Inherent Zodiac (the 'tropical' zodiac signs), the sun passes through Scorpio in late October; whereas in terms of the star constellations, (the sidereal zodiac) the sun passes through Virgo during October.

---

[23] A third comment, "Aries: development behold or the forehead" may have survived in a distorted form. The editor of the document, published in 1972, added the comment, "this probably should read: a *developed beholding or the forehead.*" But this suggestion still leaves the comment unclear.

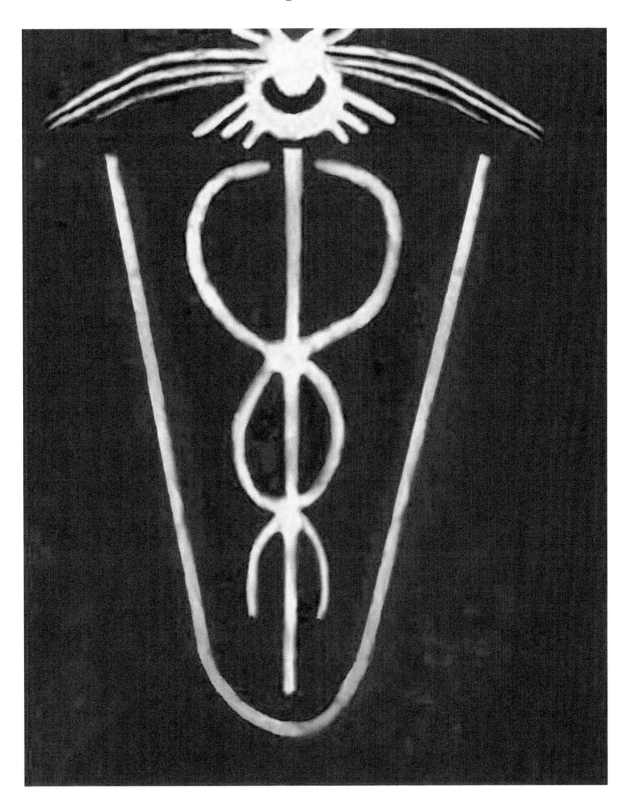

This image is positioned near to the graphic for the ancient Aquarian phase, and thus points towards the next zodiac Age, that of Aquarius.

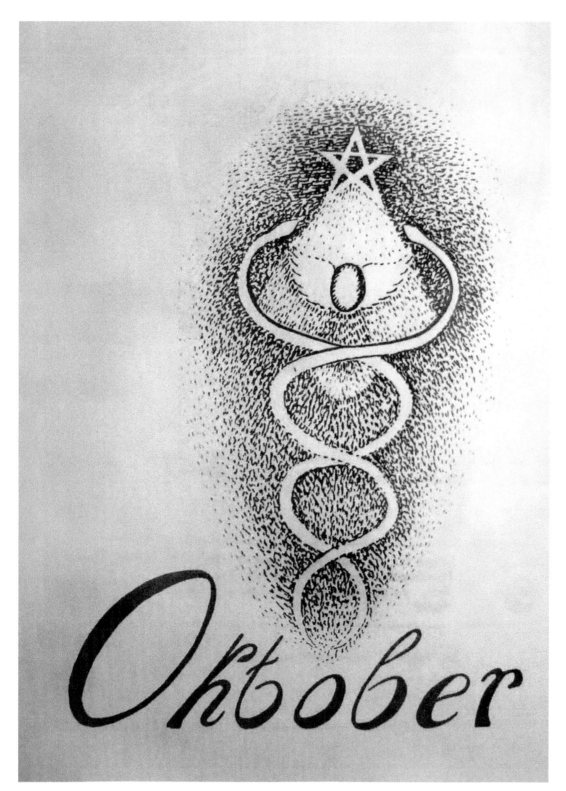

This caduceus-like graphic for the autumn points towards the coming
Christmas / Holy Nights of the northern hemisphere.

Before consider this intriguing image, we should note that there are four other illustrations prominently placed in the Calendar, but it is difficult to relate these to the cycle of the sun's movement through the year. It appears that this book does not incorporate a similar feature to that of the Stuttgart painting, which is encompassed by images of the four key signs of Taurus, Leo, Scorpio and Aquarius. In the Calendar there is a drawing of a pentagram with a radiant field around it, for December, which we could see as a reference to the Holy Nights or Christmas-time of the northern hemisphere.

There is in fact a drawing of a bull and also of a lion, and these would in theory relate to the tropical (or 'inherent') zodiac, but only if we assume that an error was made by the publisher. Because the bull image is placed for August and the lion for April; if these are reversed, they would then relate to the zodiac **signs** of Taurus and Leo, in which the sun enters in those months, (but not the constellations). And although a drawing of an eagle (for Scorpio) is placed in the book, it is placed in June when the sun is nowhere near Scorpio, in either zodiac. Furthermore, there is no image for February, the time when the sun enters Aquarius. So the overall situation regarding these four images is unclear. However, since this caduceus drawing is placed in October, it may relate to Scorpio.

So what does this image mean? The two snakes in this Caduceus swirl upwards towards what is really a sun-disk. So it is a metamorphosis of the ancient, venerable symbol of the winged sun-disk, which in ancient art was placed on the top of the staff of Mercury (or Caduceus). But also here this disk itself is enveloped in a field of spiritual energy which proceeds from a pentagram. The important point here is that, this same pentagram is the main feature of the December image, which obviously signals the approach of Christmas. And Christmas in the northern hemisphere is the time of the Holy Nights or Yuletide in that hemisphere.

So this image, like the Caduceus image in Stuttgart, is pointing towards the future. But in the Calendar, 'the future' means the next few months; the feature is pointing out that in the darkness of autumn, when Scorpio forces (in the northern hemisphere) are activated, the soul can work towards the Holy Nights. In the winter-time the divine forces from the indwelling Christ help the human spirit, represented by the pentagram, to strengthen and become radiant.

So the caduceus in the Calendar is pointing to the birth of the Spiritual-self in the coming winter Holy Nights, while the caduceus in the Stuttgart ceiling is pointing to the birth of the Spiritual-self from the higher consciousness that the more advanced souls can develop for the coming zodiac Age of the future.

Appendix   Imma von Eckhardtstein

Baroness Imma von Eckhardtstein was born on 5th November 1871 in Luneville, France. Only a little is known about her childhood and youth. She grew up in cultured circumstances, and dedicated herself, with her earnest, but equally lively nature, to Art. At the beginning of the 20th century she lived in the artist colony Worpswede near Bremen. She met with Rudolf Steiner in 1904 – in her 33rd year – and this signified to her the "experience of recognizing the Teacher". From this moment on, she committed herself with her whole heart to his work. In 1909 Steiner entrusted to her the work of artistically arranging the rooms of the Berlin Branch of the Anthroposophical Society. With the inaugural performances of the Mystery Plays in Munich, she had a major role as the person responsible for the design of the costumes, both in the rehearsals and in the performances.

In the spring of 1911 she accompanied Rudolf Steiner and Marie von Sivers on a rest and recuperation holiday to Portorose near Trieste. Here she placed the question to Rudolf Steiner as to how could a calendar based on spiritual-scientific principles, be created and graphically illustrated. In response he gave to her the task of living into the zodiac's influences. She was to intensely picture to herself the zodiac constellation and in inner peacefulness await the astral images which would then arise. Late in 1911 Rudolf Steiner gave her the task of painting the cupola of the room for the Esoteric School in Stuttgart. She died in 1930.

(Adapted from a brief biographical article written by Linda Blumenthal, on the anthroposophical internet site www.kulturimpuls.org.)

Chapter 2 Exploring the zodiac drawings in the 1912/13 Calendar

The 1912/13 Calendar was published in 1912, together with the Soul Calendar, which is a set of 52 seasonal meditative verses, in the same book. At the top of each page was a black & white zodiac image, drawn by Imma von Eckhardtstein. These drawings did draw some criticism, as some of them were not as successful as the paintings for the Stuttgart building. The sequence of the zodiac images corresponded to the sun's movement through the constellations, not through the zodiac signs (or the 'tropical' inherent zodiac). In this chapter, we will follow the same sequence as the Calendar, which starts with the month of April, when the sun is still in Pisces, and then later moves through to Aries, etc. Where the drawings are very similar to the painted scenes in Stuttgart, we will be making only a brief comment on them; see illustrations 21 -26.

PISCES
The drawing for Pisces is very similar to the Stuttgart ceiling image.

ARIES
The drawing for Aries is quite different to that painted in Stuttgart. It seems that the artist may have misunderstood what was meant, whereas in Stuttgart she has followed the simple sketch of Rudolf Steiner closely.

GEMINI
The drawing for the Calendar is very similar to that for Stuttgart, perhaps not as accomplished; but we can note that Rudolf Steiner did not make any sketch of this for her. Whatever he told her is unknown, and her notes appear to be conclusions she had drawn from his brief comments. But as we considered these in Chapter 1, Rudolf Steiner did enter a few words into a note-book; "small children, the physical weakness is mutually supported through spiritual strength".

TAURUS
The drawing in the Calendar for Taurus is very similar to that for Stuttgart, of the throat chakra.

CANCER
The drawing in the Calendar for Cancer is very different to that for the Stuttgart ceiling, for here the artist has worked freely with one part of the sketch Rudolf Steiner made for her, whilst in Stuttgart she worked with another part of the sketch. This drawing in the Calendar is attempting to depict the formation of the etheric chakra-column to the right of an astral chakra-column. As we noted earlier, this condition won't be a normal feature of human beings for many millennia, except for initiates. On one occasion Rudolf Steiner revealed that then the human being shall have power over their astral body to a very high degree, and people shall then,

> "withdraw the essence of their astral forces, the 'kundalini fire', from their tenuous physical body and simultaneously open this to streams of energy which come from within one's own astral nature and which then engage with that which is streaming into

the aura from outside; whereas now the aura is simply exposed to that which streams towards it..."[24]

He proceeds to comment that in "the sixth Large Epoch people will have within their physical body, an astral body, which they can then so utilise."

LEO
The drawing in the Calendar for Leo is very similar to that of the image painted in Stuttgart, of the heart chakra.

VIRGO
In the Calendar a very different image was drawn to that in Stuttgart. Rudolf Steiner also gave indications for the colours to be used, which is intriguing, since the drawings were all in black & white. See Appendix One for a coloured version. This image, even more than the painting on the Stuttgart ceiling, alludes to religious imagery, especially that of the Virgin Mary. But in Chapter We were able to confirm that the term 'Sophia' does not refer to a goddess, in the popular religious-mystical sense; that is, Sophia is not a tangible goddess who can appear to saints and overshadow someone. But now we look at this little-understood situation again, to bring more clarity to this theme.

It is commonly understood that in ancient Egypt the initiates did use the term Isis for a goddess, and images of Isis holding the baby Horus are well known. So what does Rudolf Steiner mean when he states that this term is not about a goddess? We noted in Chapter 1 that Rudolf Steiner taught, "Isis is the personified All-wisdom of *our* world...in her true figure, Isis is permeating the entire cosmos...she is that which shines radiantly towards us in many auric colours from the cosmos...". Here he means that creation, as experienced by a person developing higher consciousness, takes on a radiant, en-souled quality. From these words it is already clear that no goddess is involved, as Rudolf Steiner is pointing out that the term Isis refers to the living etheric-astral cosmos, and the reason is that it is precisely this wonderful vista which the Spiritual-self consciousness – called Isis – allows one to perceive. Amongst the Greeks, it was Eratosthenes (200BC) and Avienus (AD 350) who identified Sophia with Isis.

For the sake of clarity, it must also be noted that in his lectures on the search for the new Isis, Rudolf Steiner does refer to a specific goddess which the Egyptians called Isis. But this is the only occasion in the sixteen references where this occurs, and it is not relevant to these zodiac images, and not relevant to our theme. He points out that in a very high spiritual experience, an ancient Egyptian initiate could experience a mysterious, remote deity "on the furthest shore of existence..... from whom warmth and light for the existence of the innermost existence of the human soul, emanates".[25] But we can clearly confirm that although the Egyptians also used the term Isis in this rare way, it was usually a term for the Spiritual-self of the acolyte, "...(Isis is) the eternal-feminine in our soul..."[26] All other references from Rudolf Steiner to the term Isis describe it as meaning the Spirit-self.

He points out that the idea of a specific goddess is also wrong because Isis in Egypt had three distinct forms, each one of which was a symbol of a multitude of divine beings. One form is that of a mother with the Horus child, which he described as showing the Spiritual-Self, nurturing the evolving of the Life-Spirit. The second form is where she has cow horns and a

---

[24] From an intimate-circle lecture, archive document, 1903.
[25] In a lecture 5th Feb 1913, in *The Mysteries of the East and of Christianity*, (GA 144).
[26] In a lecture 5th Feb 1913, GA 57 p.385 and of 28th Mar 1907, in GA 55.

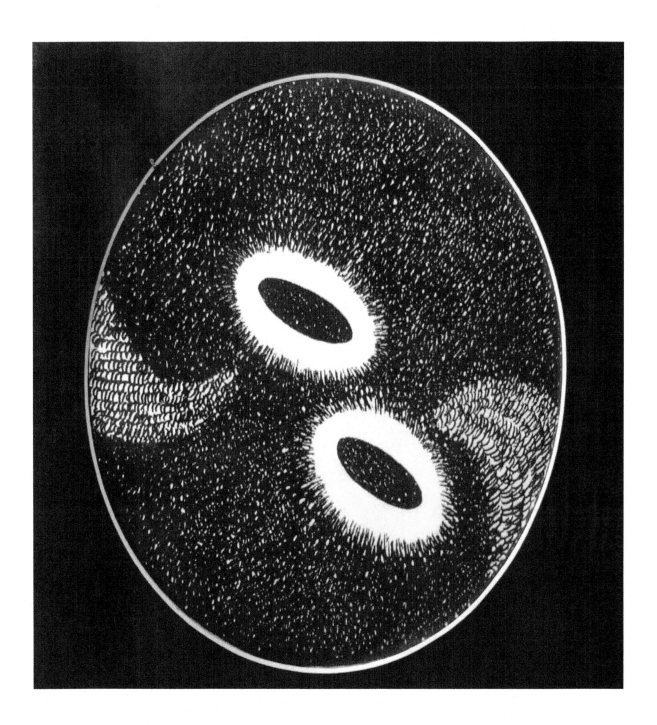

Similar to the Stuttgart graphic for Pisces, this depicts two human beings, in terms of the primordial oval body form of the Polarian Age.

This depicts the same theme as the Stuttgart graphic, but not as successfully. It portrays a future age when Aries forces shall allow seership to occur as a natural gift.

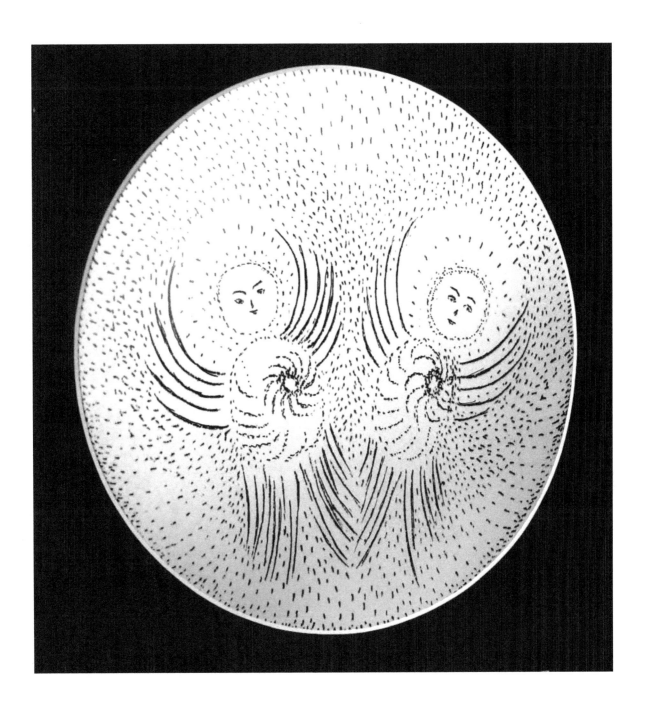

Similar to the graphic in the Stuttgart ceiling, this drawing depicts what could be described as two 'star-children' of a future Age.

Similar to the graphic for the Stuttgart ceiling, it depicts a future age when the throat chakra is fully developed amongst human beings.

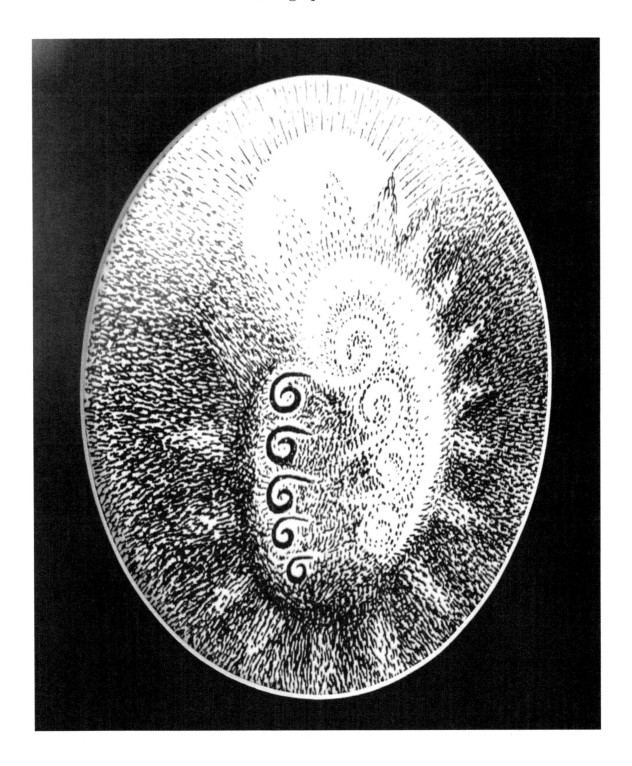

This outstanding graphic presents a view of the future human being when an etheric chakra column has formed and bridged across to the astral chakras

This drawing presents a variation of the graphic from Stuttgart, depicting the out-flow of old, lower astral forces and the consequent development of the heart chakra.

globe (the world-sphere) on her head, as well as vulture wings and she is passing an ankh to Horus. Rudolf Steiner described this as the "expression of the creating activity going on in the world." Thirdly, there is a very little known, very potent, stern image of Isis as a lion-headed deity, seated on a throne and holding a staff of power. Rudolf Steiner describes this as "the third stage of the human soul, one which can not be expressed in human terms."[27] These three images represent the three-fold human spirit and also the various divine beings behind these germinal capacities of humanity.

Rudolf Steiner further explained that Isis or Sophia was regarded as 'virginal' because, the Spirit-self was viewed as virginal, that is, it is not derived from the parents, or one's own astrality ...it is fresh and pure, from the divine realms.[28] Thus in anthroposophy, Sophia is understood to mean our own Spirit-self, and not a goddess; and this is the situation with the Virgin Mary. Thus the conclusion that a goddess 'Sophia' existed, in the more tangible sense of a distinct entity, quite often visible to various seers and saints, is not what Rudolf Steiner taught. And secondly that this supposed being existed in the soul of the Virgin Mary, is in opposition to what Rudolf Steiner's research revealed, (see Appendix Five for more about this).

So the image in the Calendar is showing the Spiritual-self in a different context to that of the Stuttgart ceiling, see Illustration 27. It shows us the Spiritual-self with also the germinal beginning of the Life-spirit (the child). At her feet is the moon, in which is a face of a man, with a somewhat negative quality to it. This alludes to the Woman with the moon at her feet, as described in the Apocalypse, and this is an image of a soul who has removed the lower astral substances from itself (the face in the moon). In other words, this is a person who has achieved the Spiritual-self. Her golden crown and golden ornament are signs of regal status in statues; here they no doubt point to the Spiritual-self as a high and noble reality.

There is one more, unusual occasion when Rudolf Steiner was referring to Sophia as a kind of being; and that is in regard to anthroposophy and 'anthroposophia'. This reference does not contradict what is said here, see Appendix Five.

LIBRA
In Chapter 1 we noted that the Libra image from Stuttgart was speaking about the dawn of the ego-sense, in the Atlantean Age. The drawing made for the Calendar is very similar to the Stuttgart image, although the traditional symbol for Libra is more clearly seen here. We noted that in the old Libran phase, the cosmic Christ and others of the Spirits of Form (or Exousiai) rayed their influences into humanity especially at that time, from the sun-sphere. This process was undertaken to ensure that the ego-sense, as it consolidated itself in humanity, would retain an inherent connection to the Spiritual-Self. This dawning of the ego-sense is being likened here to a sunrise, to the sun rising over the horizon; see illustration 28. The cross in the sphere of the Earth, made prominent by a bright shield-shaped area, is telling the viewer that this Atlantean ego-enhancing process will be greatly affirmed by the deed of Christ on Golgotha. Through the effect of the Christ-light permeating the Earth, humanity is being offered the opportunity to spiritualize the ego. The deed on Golgotha is then another, a stronger sun-rise event for earthly humanity. This perspective is embodied in a verse from Rudolf Steiner:

---

[27] ibid., p. 383.
[28] See lecture 5th Nov. 1906 (in GA 94) and in GA 180 p 29 re Pallas Athene, and GA 97 lects. 3rd Feb. 1907, 2nd.Dec.1906, 17th Mar. 1907.

This graphic is strikingly different from the one for the Stuttgart ceiling, by depicting the 'Sophia' or Spiritual-soul in terms of the inner quality of the person, rather than the vivified, spirit-permeated external world.

Sunrise of humanity's earthly evolving –
this is the secret on the hill of Golgotha;
this morning-dawn rays forth in the light of Christmas.
In this dawn's gentle light may the soul revere
spirit-kindred fountain and power of existence of her own being.

SCORPIO
The drawing for Scorpio is presenting the same dynamic as found in the Stuttgart ceiling.

SAGITTARIUS
The artwork for this sign in the Calendar is striking and very different from that on the Stuttgart ceiling. Here the artist has worked with the reference by Rudolf Steiner, about the graphics for Sagittarius, to a denizen of the world of faery, called a faun. He wrote, "{depict} this faun motif in such a way that it spiritualizes itself out its spinal column." Rudolf Steiner also commented that in this Lemurian time, "{on the} Earth, solid matter separates out {from the 'water-air' environment}". We noted earlier how for human beings at this time, the process of incarnating was getting difficult. This drawing points to the elemental forces which were then accreting in the human being, and contributing to the growth of the Double. As such, its theme is similar to that of the image for Sagittarius in the blue window.

CAPRICORN
The drawing for this sign in the Calendar is very striking, and quite different from that for Capricorn on the Stuttgart ceiling. A note from Rudolf Steiner for this graphic states, "ever more water...if condensed to the Earth, stays away".[29] This appears to mean that, if the human being finds its body is condensing to the stage of matter or 'earth' as the alchemists would say, the soul stays away. These brief words are referring to the staying away from a life on Earth of many souls, as our planet condenses into matter. Several other notes from Rudolf Steiner help greatly to explain this image. He comments that "the human being was indeed rather animal-like {in its appearance} but having its own soul". We have already noted that Rudolf Steiner has used the term 'faun-like' for the human being in this time. But he also briefly noted that the physical body was at that time separable, because it could separate into three sections. He also wrote that the graphics should, "from one side, show the origin {of this body} from the water." Neither the faun-face in the Calendar, nor the face interwoven with the watery-ethereal environment, painted on the Stuttgart ceiling, were sketched by Rudolf Steiner. But both of the graphics appear to be very evocative.

AQUARIUS
Finally, the drawing for Aquarius is presenting the same dynamic as found in the Stuttgart ceiling. The drawing is obviously presenting a more living form of the human being than the image on the Stuttgart ceiling. Neither the somewhat human form drawn for the Calendar, nor the more stylized features painted on the Stuttgart ceiling, follow any sketch from Rudolf Steiner. But, as with the artwork for Capricorn, both of these appear to me to very successful.

---

[29] In the English edition of the 1912/13 Calendar, ed./trans. C. Bamford, the deciphering of these notes is not accurate; ("...*if it can disappear on the earth it stays away*). The most unclear German word here is, "verdichtet".

A striking version of the graphic for the Libran phase when the ego-sense
began to dawn as a cosmic balance held sway in the zodiac influences.

This drawing for Scorpio presents in a different style, the same theme as that of the Stuttgart graphic, as no sketches for this phase exist from Rudolf Steiner.

A variation from the Stuttgart ceiling of the graphic for the Sagittarius
phase, when humanity strove to penetrate into the more dense earth sphere.

This image depicts, in a different way to the Stuttgart ceiling image, the difficulty for the human being to incarnate into the more earthly body of the late Hyperborean Age.

This image depicts the struggle of the primordial human being to stay in a separate body amidst the turbulent waves of the Hyperborean Age.

Chapter 3 Exploring the scene carved in a Goetheanum blue window

The stained glass windows in the great hall of the Goetheanum in Dornach, Switzerland, are wonderful to contemplate. This building is the international centre for conferences and Courses based on the work of Rudolf Steiner; it has nine, large stained-glass windows in its walls. (A comprehensive guide to all nine windows is available in my book, *The Meaning of the Goetheanum Windows*.) The blue window in the south, in its central panel, depicts the twelve zodiac energies. But the way that Rudolf Steiner has chosen to depict these is intriguing. Some of the scenes here are not similar at all to the 1912/13 Calendar images nor the Stuttgart ceiling, whereas other scenes are similar to these, and greatly help us to understand them, see illustrations 33-35.

PISCES
Most prominent in the blue window is image for Pisces, at the bottom left-hand corner. This prominence means that this series of zodiac images starts with Pisces, as did the Stuttgart images. But with the Stuttgart images, this is because the beginning of humanity's evolutionary journey was the underlying leitmotif. However in the blue window, that is not the case at all. This series starts with Pisces, because this is where we are now – we are in the Age of Pisces. Of course this statement applies only to the northern hemisphere, but some 93% of the world's population live there, and as a result culturally, it has probably had more impact on humanity since AD 1413, when this Age began.

This image shows the Earth down below and then the moon, next to which are the two fishes of the traditional Pisces symbol. Above is a human being with the stars of Pisces shown outside, and also in the part of the body which they govern. We note here that in the blue window, the position of the stars of each constellation inside the body, for each of the five 'night-time or 'descending' signs are not so accurately shown, they are spread out into neighbouring parts of the body, that is, those from the sign of Pisces back to Scorpio. The same cannot be said for the seven 'day-time' or 'ascending' signs, the stars here are mainly positioned accurately. We also note that the stars of each zodiacal sign do not attempt to closely replicate the shape of the constellation.

One gains the impression too, that with the moon underneath the feet of the person, it is as if the moon is under the power of the two fish. These of course represent the qualities of Pisces. The image of the moon under one's feet is found in the New Testament, in the book of Revelation, where it represents the overcoming of the lower self. The moon symbolizes the old Moon aeon during which a base, primitive astrality came into humanity. In the Gospel of St. John, the remarkable scene is given at his depiction of the washing of the disciple's feet by Jesus shortly before he was arrested.

This event is teaching a lesson about the humility and sense of service needed by those who are in authority, spiritually. But as I mention in *The Hellenistic Mysteries & Christianity*, this is also a zodiacal process, in which the same lesson is being given for people attuned to the Christ-impulse in the Age of Pisces. So the lesson here in this window appears to be that in our Age of Pisces, the task is to respond to this call for a selfless, service-oriented attitude to life; and hence the moon is waning in this scene. (As we shall see later, the neighbouring image is also about zodiacal Ages, the Age of Aquarius.)

ARIES TAURUS GEMINI
We then move up to the image for Aries and to the next one up, Taurus, and above that, Gemini. These three images are entirely different to that of Pisces; they are straightforward

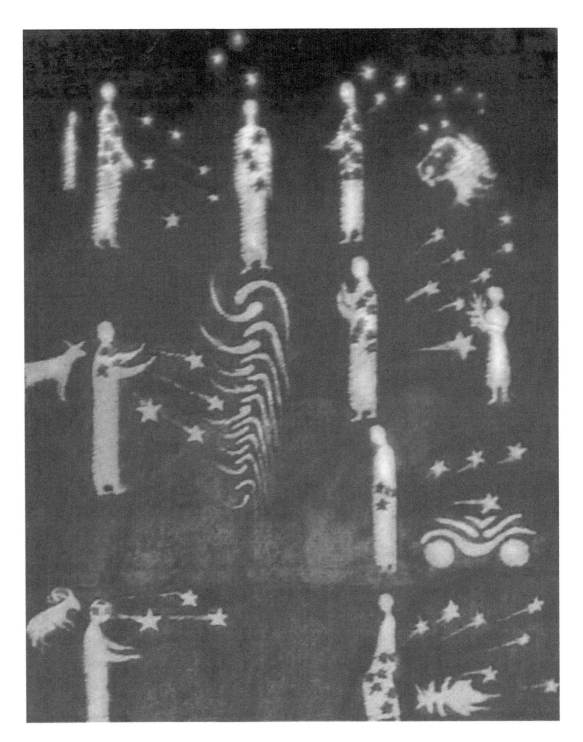

These images start with Aries (bottom left) and going up in an arc and down, and end with Scorpio (bottom right).

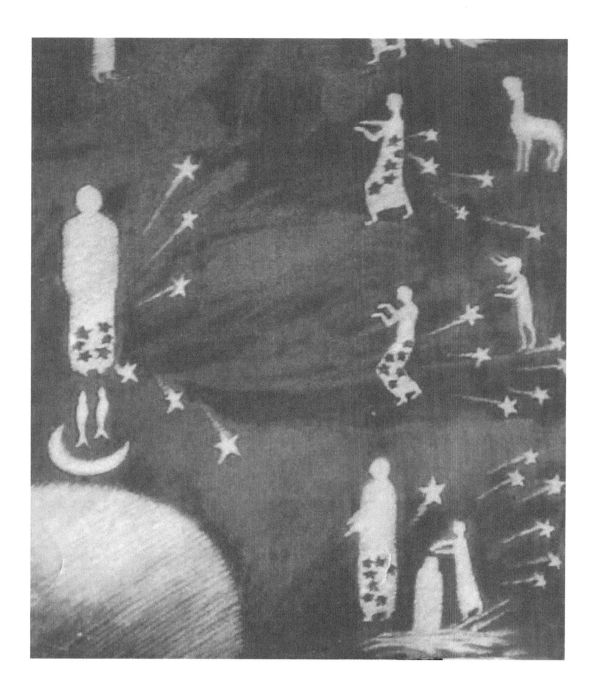

On the lower left is Pisces (with the Earth below and the moon); on the right, from top downwards, is Sagittarius, Capricorn and Aquarius.

traditional depictions. They each simply show a person, with the stars of that constellation placed in the relevant part of the body, as well as outside it. And each image includes a small depiction of what that sign is related to: a ram for Aries, a bull for Taurus and a second person for Gemini.

CANCER

But when we gaze at the image for Cancer, we see a very different scene. In addition to a person with the stars depicted outside and inside, there is also a prominent symbolic form. From our explorations with the image for Cancer on the Stuttgart ceiling and in the Calendar, we can see that this blue window image is somewhat similar. But it is not a second, etheric column of chakras. Rather it is a series of interlocking spirals, which form in fact a long vertical column-like structure. But it is also a wonderful metamorphosis of the traditional double-spiral symbol for Cancer, and it also has some similarity to the thoracic cage, the area of the body that Cancer governs. This cage is the series of interlocking rib bones that protect the organs in the upper trunk of the body. So it is a figure that draws our attention to the future vertical column of etheric forces, depicted in the other zodiacs, but also alludes to the Cancerian symbol and the spiralling chest cage.

LEO VIRGO LIBRA

Now we again encounter three images that are traditional. Leo with a lion and the stars outside and inside: Virgo with its stars, and holding its traditional sheaf of grain, and thirdly, Libra with its stars and an unusual graphic which alludes to the body keeping itself in balance, with a freely interpreted depiction of some of the bones in the hip area. The shape of this skeletal feature also has a slight resemblance to the traditional symbol for Libra.

CAPRICORN

But when we gaze at the image for Scorpio, for Sagittarius and for Capricorn, we encounter some very striking features. To understand these three, we need to start with the image for Capricorn, as these three images, like those of the Calendar and from Stuttgart, refer back to the evolution of humanity in the distant past. In the Capricorn image, we see a human being with the stars outside and inside. But behind this person is positioned an unpleasant sprite, or similar being, that is, an etheric or astral entity. Where does it come from? We noted earlier how when Capricorn is the sun-sign (or the rising sign, to a lesser extent) then that person has the strongest ego-sense, and hence, if not a more evolved soul, has the most self-centred, hardened egoism.

It was in the old Hyperborean Age that the Capricorn phase of our evolution occurred, and it was then for the first time, that matter began to incorporate itself into the tenuous physical-etheric body of human beings. Rudolf Steiner refers to this as the "marriage of the sentient-soul with the matrix kama-substance". 'Kama' is a Sanskrit term for base astrality. By this expression he means the degraded ahrimanic etheric-astral energies now pervading the globe, and now permeating the primitive human being. **This is the cosmic birth-hour of the ahrimanic Double, or lower self.**[30] The forming of matter is carried out by gnomes and Ahriman has a role in this activity of condensing lifeless minerals out of the ether, making where possible, gnomes into ahrimanic beings (the 'dark elves' of the Edda). In this Age, as we noted in Chapter 1, dragon-like or reptilian aquatic creatures began to appear; these are the signature of Ahriman.

---

[30] The Double began to be accreted, or rather drawn into our soul, into our ether body and later, into the material substances of our physical body. This is the meaning of a line in Lesson One of the 1924 meditative sessions; "your earthly time has placed these in you..." (not, as is officially translated: "your cosmic time".)

A Capricorn person need not have a worse Double than other people, but as a generalized statement, it appears that amongst people of the same degree of evolvement from the various zodiac signs the Capricorn Double is more potent, that is, less latent. Obviously a criminal person of any zodiac sign, next to an evolved Capricorn, has a more potent Double. The ahrimanic Double is predisposed to lying, to cold, heartless, callous behaviour, and in essence, it smothers the voice of the conscience. We should note here that an evolved Capricorn has a very high capacity for spirituality, for their strong ego-sense, when the self is consciously moving towards spirituality, becomes deeply ethical.

SAGITTARIUS

In the Sagittarius image, we see a human being with the stars outside and inside. But behind this person is positioned an unpleasant etheric or astral entity creature, similar to a centaur. The centaur is, in Rudolf Steiner's teachings, a deeply malignant being; it is how the lower self or Double appears, "it is an etheric being...it is equipped with all the savage instincts of the animals".[31] He also taught that the human being in Lemuria was, in appearance, slightly similar to a centaur.[32] So in this image another way of depicting the lower self is presented; and it was in the Lemurian Age that the Sagittarian phase of our evolution took place. It was during this phase that the densification of the Earth began to stifle its tenuous living organism.

The absorption of matter intensified in the human being, and then both luciferic and ahrimanic influences grew stronger. It would soon be necessary for the moon to be cast out of the Earth. See Rudolf Steiner's *An Outline of Esoteric Science*, for more about this. So this image, like the one for Capricorn, alludes to the Double, and in particular, the Age when this was taking further hold of the human being.

SCORPIO

As we noted in Chapter 1, it was in the Scorpio phase of our evolution, during the second half of the Lemurian Age, that humanity split into the two sexes. We discussed then how this led to sensual desires, but also to a capacity for an individualized consciousness. The image here shows, as with the other eleven images, a human being with the stars outside and inside. But here also an unpleasant astral creature is depicted, which seems to be moving towards the person in a somewhat threatening way. This is surely another depiction of the Double or lower self, even though the creature it is not actually a scorpion, the usual symbol of (lower) Scorpio energies. It is similar, yet different in various ways to a scorpion. We can conclude that this entity represents the lower energies which gained access to human beings through the Scorpio phase of our evolution when sexuality arose.

AQUARIUS

Finally, we come to the image for Aquarius, at the bottom right side of the window, showing a human being with stars outside and inside, as seen throughout this panel. But in addition here we see a baptism scene; someone is baptising another person, who appears to be partially immersed in water. This immediately reminds us of the New Testament event where Jesus was baptised by John the Baptist, in the river Jordan. But looking at the image carefully, we now note that the second person, the one being baptised, is not actually immersed in the water in the way that is done in a religious baptism rite; this person is in water only ankle deep. The ankles are the part of the body governed by the forces streaming in from Aquarius.

To begin our exploration of the message within this carved glass scene, we start with noting words of Rudolf Steiner in a lecture from 1905. He tells his audience that in the Sixth post-

---

[31] Lect. 6th Nov. 1917, in GA 178.
[32] A remark in GA 100 p.292 & Egyptian Myths, (GA 106), lect. 9th Sept 1908.

Atlantean Age, John the Baptist will be spiritually guiding human beings, bringing a new, esoteric awareness of Christianity.[33] We also need to note that Rudolf Steiner spoke of John the Baptist as an initiated person, involved with the Essenes. He had an Aquarian initiation: that is, an initiation involving beings of the Sun and of the constellation of Aquarius. So he became a spiritual teacher initiated into the ability to offer an initiation process through being baptised in water, a process which can loosen the connection of the etheric body to the physical body. This gave the acolyte a clearer awareness of their life's course ethically so far, and hence what they could achieve spiritually if they so decided to undergo an inner change and seek the spirit. Such teachers were referred as "water-men initiators".[34]

As a result of this occurring to John the Baptist, an angel could incorporate itself in his aura. This angel had the task of announcing, through John, the advent of the Christ. Indeed the prophecy of Malachi (3:1) "Behold, I will send my messenger {that is, an angel} and he shall prepare the way for me" is an indication that an angelic being was overshadowing the Baptist. Rudolf Steiner explained that it was the task of that angel to help humankind toward true, individual ego-hood, which would become possible once the Christ-being united to the Earth.

Now, we need to recall that Aquarius is an **air** sign, not a water sign; but water can symbolize the ethers, which also flow and surge and swirl in a manner similar to water. (Water is itself condensed out of the water-ether, or 'tone-ether'.) So we can conclude that this scene does allude, in the first instance, to the task of John the Baptist, in baptizing Jesus. But it also points towards the metamorphosis of that deed for John. The result of this will be that his future task, in the Sixth Post-Atlantean Age, will be to 'baptise' people into the Christ-light by helping them to become sensitive to the ethers, to receiving the Christ-Word as it resounds in the ethers. And this will be a significant dynamic underlying the golden age of cultural-spiritual blossoming in that Age. It will lead humanity further towards a true individual ego-hood of a 'Christed' nature.

 Summarising the over-all structure of these twelve scenes in the blue window, we have:

Pisces	= the present Age
Aries, Taurus, Gemini	= 3 traditional symbols, no time-frame
Cancer	= the far future & the arising of a spiritualized etheric-astral nature
Leo, Virgo, Libra	= 3 traditional symbols, no time-frame
Scorpio, Sagittarius, Capricorn	= 3 about the remote past & the arising of the Double
Aquarius	= the near future, the Baptist in the Aquarian Age

This structure is intriguing, and in contemplating it, I gain the impression that it is designed to communicate various truths to the observer. One is about an important task of the person seeking spiritual wisdom today, to continue to be aware of the high creativity and selflessness of the divine beings, active from the zodiac, as they create humanity. Another truth concerns the Double and how the journey through the material phase of Earth existence, in many lives, has brought this about. Also, there is a message about the near future, the Age of Aquarius wherein the immortal higher ego can start to emerge as the Spiritual-self, and how John the Baptist will be active then spiritually. It is also the case that in its structure, this sequence of zodiac images places the near future Age of Aquarius close to our present time of Pisces, thereby forming a kind of bridge between the present, over to the future goals.

Another possible feature
The blue window appears possibly to have another veiled feature to it. We have often referred to the division of the zodiac energies into 5 and 7. In this window, there are 5 images on the left, including and strongly bordered by, Cancer. Then on the right of the long dividing effect of the spiral column in Cancer, there are seven images. Whether this has any significance is unclear.

---

[33] Lect. 3rd Oct. 1905 (GA 93a).
[34] Lect. 12th Dec. 1910, (GA 124) Excurse in background to Gospel of St. Mark.

Chapter 4 : Contemplations of the Zodiac Sun-Signs by Rudolf Steiner:

THE   TWELVE   MOODS

INTRODUCTION

Origin and Purpose
In 1911 the new zodiac images for the Stuttgart building were designed and in 1913, the drawings for the 1912/13 Calendar were published. Then in 1915, Rudolf Steiner worked on the stained glass window designs for the Goetheanum, including the zodiac scenes for the blue window. In this same year he also wrote a series of twelve verses to contemplate the zodiacal signs, and for each of these he created a eurythmy form. On August 29th 1915, Rudolf Steiner read these poems out in the context of training eurythmists to perform them, and they were eventually performed in 1920.

They became known as the 'Twelve Moods'. In this chapter, I am presenting here a new translation of these verses and commenting on them **as sun-sign contemplations**. I regard them as meditative verses that present the nature of the personality which results from having a particular zodiac sign (also known as a sun-sign) in the horoscope. These poems portray in a deep, meditative way, the primary soul qualities and challenges that a person's sun-sign, (or rising-sign), bestows upon a person.

Rudolf Steiner, from his initiation wisdom, speaks in these verses about the nature of the astrological signs, clarifying what the challenges are to personal development for people born under each of the twelve signs. However, each verse also alludes to the negative traits of the zodiac sign personality, as well as pointing out the nobler qualities that a zodiac sign can bestow. That they have not been thought of as connected to the sun-signs in anthroposophical circles is due, it seems, to an attitude that Rudolf Steiner was against astrology. However, Rudolf Steiner was not against **an anthroposophically deepened** working with astrology. But he was not strongly supportive of the astrology which was practiced in his life-time; early 20th century astrology is now regarded as too simplistic.[35]

So, in the course of giving his introductory address, prior to introducing these verses on 29th August 1915, Rudolf Steiner specifically states that he does not want his work to be categorised by the world as 'astrological'. He emphasizes this point, telling his audience that with regard to these verses it is not a question of "...imitating the materialistic and superstitious astrologers' and also that spiritual science is (by some people) lumped together with foolish mystical strivings of the present time, yet it has nothing to do with it at all. Spiritual Science wants to have nothing to do with the dilettantism of modern astrologers".[36] It is precisely these statements which reveal that these verses are what we can indeed today call 'astrological', but should not be thought of as 'astrological' in the sense of the elementary astrology practised around 1900 (and earlier).

As I show in Appendix Three, in a lecture from 1911, the only lecture Steiner ever gave which focuses on horoscopes, he affirmed the remarkable power and value of competent horoscope

---

[35] For example, an astrological manual, produced about 1910 by an English Theosophist, tells the reader that "...if you have Mars in Cancer then you are "a servile, unfortunate creature..." whereas if Mars is located in Gemini, "...you are generally unfortunate in all undertakings." These statements today are known to be so limited and narrow as to be wrong; *The manual of Astrology*, by 'Sepharial' (Walter Old), 1864-1929.
[36] From the Address on 29th August 1915, GA 277-a p.159.

interpretation, using the 'tropical zodiac', (not the 'sidereal') as carried out over the last two or more millennia to delineate the human personality. He states,

The horoscope which has been cast for thousands of years for the individual corresponded with infallible exactitude to the four lower parts of the soul...[37]

The expression, the 'four lower parts' means the fourfold human being (physical, etheric astral and ego), not the three higher spiritual parts of the human being, which are as yet scarcely developed. So it quite consistent when, in a lecture from 1915, Rudolf Steiner taught that astrological analysis is just a dilettante thing, unless carried out by a person who strives after wisdom. If this is the case, then it is a very valid and valuable thing,

> "...I have often said, astrology is either the purest amateurism or it can only be achieved as the end result of a really deep immersion in spiritual-scientific studies and cognizance...it demands from those who practise it, a higher spiritual faculty of cognition."[38]

This in effect means that the horoscope interpretation calls for wisdom, for being spiritually intuitive. Modern astrology is psychologically oriented, not superstitious, and when it is deepened through a competent grasp of anthroposophical wisdom, it becomes a profoundly valuable tool for personal self-knowledge and for counsellors to use in their work. My book, the *Horoscope Handbook – a Rudolf Steiner Approach*, is the result of decades of work in horoscope analysis for clients, in which anthroposophical wisdom is merged with modern psychologically-aware astrological insights. This book details just how accurate a portrayal of a person's psychological qualities can be when one interprets the horoscope in this way. For more about Rudolf Steiner's substantial yet discreet involvement with astrological research and the tropical or inherent zodiac, that is the zodiac signs, see Appendix Two.

A contemplation of these twelve verses from Rudolf Steiner reveal that they are a profound presentation of the influence bestowed on us from our zodiac sun-sign or our rising-sign. In this way, the verses become a pathway towards personal development.[39] They caution about the negative tendencies that a zodiac sign gives and also deepen our awareness of its positive qualities. If we seek to interpret the message in these verses, on the basis of a clear understanding of astrology, we can gain a great deal of self-knowledge.

We learn to understand how our sun-sign or rising-sign contributes to the deepening of our personality or ego-sense. But we human beings, with our sun-sign and our horoscope, live in the solar system with its planets that move across the zodiac too. If we are fortunate enough to see the verses portrayed in eurythmy, then we can also experience, as a separate aspect of the cosmos, the presence of the seven classical 'planets' moving within each zodiac sign.

These verses are difficult to translate, as the language used in them is multi-nuanced, with many of the words here having various meanings. Thus it is imperative that the translator has a comprehensive understanding of astrology, especially of the influence of the sun-signs, to ensure an accurate choice of nuance when translating the verses. A meditative engagement with these verses can be helpful to people who yearn for a living feeling about how these energies influence the soul-life. And one does have to meditate on these verses, as their content is, to some extent, beyond an intellectual-logical approach. Such meditating is greatly assisted by the experience of seeing these verses performed in eurythmy.

---

[37] From an archive lecture, not in the German Complete Works, from Feb. 2nd 1911.
[38] In vol. 162, page 20.
[39] In the 2 earlier books on these verses, their sun-sign significance was not considered; (M.Aschenbrenner *Der Tierkreis*, Dornach 1972, and H. Erasmy, *Die Eurythmie der Zwölf Stimmungen*, Dornach, 2007.)

Which zodiac ?

Rudolf Steiner stated that these verses are best meditated upon from the 21st of a month to the 21st of the next month; and this corresponds to **the inherent zodiac,** (normally called the tropical zodiac). It does not correspond to the sidereal zodiac, made up of the star constellations. That Rudolf Steiner stated this, was formally reported in a Dornach astronomical publication, the '*Sternkalender*', of Easter, 1967/68, by Suso Vetter, the leader of the Goetheanum section for astronomy, in her article "*Die Zwölf Stimmungen von Rudolf Steiner*", (pps. 83-84). However, it is also reported that when these verses were being taught to eurythmists, Rudolf Steiner also stated that one can think of them as an (ongoing) daily cycle, starting with Aries at sunrise, and Cancer at midday, and so on. Now, it is important here to note that such a cycle does not actually exist – except for about one month in each year, when the sun is in Aries. This occurs from about March 21st to April 20th in regard to the zodiac signs, and from about 16th April to 12th May in regard to the constellations (the sidereal zodiac).

So this statement from Rudolf Steiner is referring the meditant to what we could call 'the classical, archetypal zodiac'; that is, the zodiac which is reflected in the structure of every horoscope, which starts with Aries at the eastern horizon thus governing House One, and proceeds through to Pisces as the underlying force in House Twelve.[40]

The Planetary sequence

When zodiac influences are active in a horoscope through the sun being located in a particular zodiac sign, this sign imprints specific soul qualities on that person. So a person whose sun-sign is Gemini in the inherent zodiac (or tropical zodiac) will, of course, exhibit Gemini qualities. But in addition, these verses also attempt to indicate how each of the seven planets in that zodiac sign cause a specific nuancing of those zodiac energies. The influence or colouring given to the zodiac energy by a planet is subtly indicated in these verses by dedicating each line to a particular planet in a certain sequence. The sequence is as follows, from the first to the seventh lines:

> 1: Sun
> 2: Venus
> 3: Mercury
> 4: Mars
> 5: Jupiter
> 6: Saturn
> 7: Moon

So, using the Pisces verse as an example:

SUN	In the Lost, may Loss be found,
VENUS*	In the Gain, may Gain be lost !
MERCURY*	In the grasped, may the grasping seek itself
MARS	and retain itself in the Retained !
JUPITER	Through Becoming, raised to Being;
SATURN	through Being, interwoven in the Becoming !
MOON	The Loss is to be Gain in itself !

* * Note that 'Venus' here refers to the planet we call Mercury with its mercurial qualities, and 'Mercury' refers to the planet we call Venus, and its associated 'venusian' qualities. That this reversal of the names is the case here, is shown in the eurythmy form for these verses,

---

[40] For more about the archetypal zodiac, and how it surrounds the aura of each person, see my *The Horoscope Handbook - a Rudolf Steiner Approach.*

published in GA 277-a, p. 70. This question of why Rudolf Steiner has reversed the names for these two planets has long remained a riddle, causing confusion in other areas of astrological-astronomical research. However, my ebooklet, "*Mercury and Venus: the transposition of their names*", provides an answer to this theme.

The planetary sequence which is used here is unusual. It goes firstly, from the sun down towards the Earth (thus, Venus and Mercury) and then the sequence goes from Mars out to Saturn, encompassing the outer planets. Then, having arrived at the outermost of the classical planets (Saturn), the sequence moves in the polar opposite direction, going down to the Moon which is the nearest of the 'planets' to the Earth.

A word about translating Rudolf Steiner's poetic-meditative German

The German people have evolved a wonderful language in terms of subtlety of nuances capable of conveying higher ideas and also spiritual insights. One German term that occurs in these verses is "Werden" which is the opposite of "Entgehen"; these two expressions translate into English correctly only by choosing a phrase consisting of several words, not one word, namely the "coming into being" and "the going out of being", respectively. But in poetry, if one attempts to find just one word for the term, to avoid having a long phrase in a short line of poetry, then for 'Werden' as a noun, 'Becoming' is the nearest word (using a capital letter to distinguish it from its verb form). Alternative words could be: evolving, growth, or developing. So here 'Becoming' means the process of creation evolving, developing and generally coming ever more into being.

The earnest student of Rudolf Steiner has to make the effort to be at ease with some unusual English terms, or the unusual use of English, if real clarity about his teachings is sought. This means for the translator, choosing such terms as 'cosmic Becoming', instead of 'cosmic ongoing evolving/developing' or 'cosmic growth' (these are all correct, but too narrow). Consequently, there is also 'Becoming's power', 'Becoming's being', and most unusual of all, Rudolf Steiner here also uses the German equivalent of, the 'maturing of Becoming', or a 'matured Becoming'.

There is also the need to become familiar with the word 'efficacy' or 'efficacious' and 'operative' or 'operativeness'. These two terms directly and accurately translate the German words, 'wirken' (verb) or Wirkung' (noun), that are often used by Rudolf Steiner. Which one of these terms is appropriate depends on the context. Translators often choose English words that are much less appropriate, but much more familiar; such as 'work/working' or 'active/activity'. So in everyday English the term 'working' has been stretched to take over the meaning of 'efficacy'. If Rudolf Steiner teaches that something is efficacious or has efficacy, this means that it is exerting an influence which is having an effect on something. This is not the same as 'working' as when we are in our job, receiving an hourly rate of pay) or being 'active'; this is because 'activity' does not imply making a definite impact on something else.

The poetic qualities of the verses

Each verse has its own structure, and so the lines are not of equal length, nor do they have the same rhythmical form, unlike the Soul Calendar. But in each of the twelve verses, the 3rd last and second last lines strive to form rhyming couplets. The two other commentaries written about these verses don't point out that they define in a deep meditative, poetic way the nature of the sun-sign personality. Instead both focus, at least in part, on the consonants which each zodiac sign induces in our speech. However none of these verses are about the consonant-producing nature of these zodiac energies, nor do any of the verses contain a significant presence of consonants relating to each sign. For example, the verse for Leo, has no more 'd's or 't's in it than any other of the eleven verses.

Note: the 'mood' of these verses is often that of hoping or pleading that something may be achieved. This is called in grammar, the 'subjunctive' mood. So such phrases as "grasp Becoming's being" or "O radiance of being, appear" or "engender warmth of life" are really pleading that this might occur. Thus, it really means "*may* you grasp Becoming's being", etc. Where this pleading or admonition mood is not so clear, I have added the word 'may', otherwise it is to be understood that this is the case in virtually all the verses.

But sometimes individual lines are in the 'vocative' tense; the line makes a command or firm declaration. This is called the 'imperative' mood. This looks the same in German grammar as the 'subjunctive' mood. If the imperative mood is meant (giving a command), then that is made clear, usually by an exclamation mark.

Also, we note that the dates given for when the sun passes through each sign of the Inherent Zodiac (or so-called tropical zodiac) are approximate. This is because the actual dates vary each year, by one or two days.

THE TWELVE MOODS

trans. by Dr. A. Anderson   2012

ARIES   Mar 21 - Apr 20

Arise, O glow of light !	Erstehe, O Lichtesschein,
Grasp Becoming's being,	Erfasse das Werdewesen,
seize the weaving of forces,	Ergreife das Kräfteweben,
shine forth, awakening existence !	Erstrahle dich, Sein-erweckend.
through resistance, gain;	Am Widerstand gewinne,
in the flow of time, be refined !	Im Zeitenstrom zerrinne.
O shining light, remain !	O Lichteschein, verbleibe !

TAURUS   Apr 21 - May 20

Grow brighter, O radiance of being;	Erhelle dich, Wesensglanz,
dimly feel Becoming's power,	Erfühle die Werdekraft,
weave the thread of life into	Verweben den Lebensfaden
being-imbued world existence,	In Wesendes Weltensein,
in contemplative revelation,	In sinniges Offenbaren,
in radiant awareness of existence.	In leuchtendes Seins-Gewahren.
O radiance of being, appear !	O Wesensglanz, erscheine !

GEMINI   May 21 - June 21

Disclose yourself, sun-existence,	Erschliesse dich, Sonnesein,
resist the urge to rest,	Bewege den Ruhetrieb,
encompass the desire to strive	Umschliesse die Strebelust
toward mighty prevailing of life,	Zu mächtigem Lebewalten,
toward blissful world-comprehending,	Zu seligem Weltbegreifen,
toward fruitful maturing of Becoming.	Zu fruchtendem Werdereifen.
O sun-existence, persist !	O Sonnesein, verharre !

CANCER   June 22 - July 22

Thou resting luminous glow,
engender warmth of life,
make warm the life of soul,
towards empowered proving of self,
towards spiritual self-permeating,
in a tranquil bringing forth of light.
Thou luminous glow, acquire strength !

Du ruhender Leuchteglanz,
Erzeuge Lebenswärme,
Erwärme Seelenleben,
 Zu kräftigen Selbst-Bewähren,
 Zu geistigen Selbst-Durchdringen,
 In ruhigem Licht-Erbringen.
Du Leuchteglanz, erstarke !

LEO   July 23 - Aug 23

Pervade with sensory power
what the world's being has become,
and a muted sensing of being-ness within,
towards a willed decision for existence.
In flowing brightness of life,
in prevailing pain of becoming,
with senses' might, arise !

Durchströme mit Sinngewalt
Gewordenes Weltensein,
Erfühlende Wesenschaft
Zu wollendem Seinentschluss.
In strömenden Lebensschein,
In waltender Werdepein,
 Mit Sinngewalt, erstehe !

VIRGO   Aug 24 - Sept 23

Behold the realms, O soul !
May the soul take hold of realms –
may the mind comprehend being,
from powers-of-life be efficacious,
through experience of the Will, build,
trust in the blossoming of the cosmos.
O soul – cognize the beings !

Die Welten erschaue, Seele !
Die Seele ergreife Welten,
Der Geist erfasse Wesen,
Aus Lebensgewalten, wirke,
Im Willenserleben baue !
Dem Weltenerblüh'n vertraue !
O Seele, erkenne die Wesen !

LIBRA   Sept 24 - Nov 22

The realms maintain realms,
In being, being-ness is experienced,
In existence, existence is encompassed,
and being-ness makes operative being-ness
for an ongoing pouring-forth of deeds,
in tranquil world enjoyment.
O realms, uphold realms !

Die Welten erhalten Welten,
Im Wesen, erlebt sich Wesen,
Im Sein umschliesst sich Sein
Und Wesen erwirket Wesen
Zu werdendem Tatergiessen,
In ruhendem Weltgeniessen
O Welten, ertraget Welten !

SCORPIO   Oct 24 - Nov 22

Existence - it consumes being-ness,
yet in being-ness, existence is maintained.
In efficaciousness Becoming disappears,

Das Sein, es verzehrt das Wesen,
Im Wesen doch hält sich Sein.
Im Wirken entschwindet Werden,

in Becoming, efficacy abides.
In chastising cosmic prevailing,
in punishing self-forming,
being-ness maintains the beings.

Im Werden, verharret Wirken.
In strafendem Weltenwalten
In ahndenden Selbst-Gestalten
Das Wesen erhält die Wesen.

SAGITTARIUS   Nov 23 - Dec 21

Becoming attains the might of being,
into the Existing, Becoming's might dies away.
The Attained concludes striving's desire,
within the prevailing will-power of life.
In dying away, the cosmos' Prevailing matures
from within,
forms disappear in forms.
The Existing – feel the Existing !

Das Werden erreicht das Seinsgewalt,
Im Seienden erstirbt die Werdemacht.
Erreichtes beschliesst die Strebelust
In waltender Lebenswillenskraft.
Im Sterben erreift das Weltenwalten,

Gestalten verschwinden in Gestalten.
Das Seiende fühle das Seiende !

CAPRICORN   Dec 22 - Jan 19

May what is in the future rest upon what has been !
May what has been, dimly sense what is in the future
for a robust present existence.
In inner life-resistance
may cosmic-being's vigil grows strong,
may life's power to have efficacy blossom !
What has been – *endure* what is in the future !

Das Künftige ruhe auf Vergangenem
Vergangenes erfühle Künftiges
Zu kräftigem Gegenwartsein.
Im inneren Lebenswiderstand
Erstarke die Weltenwesenswacht,
Erblühe die Lebenswirkensmacht.
Vergangenes ertrage Künftiges !

AQUARIUS Jan 20 - Feb 18

May the Confined surrender to the Boundless !
What feels the lack of boundaries, may it establish
in depths boundaries for itself.
May it raise itself in the stream,
as a wave flowing away, retaining itself,
In the Becoming forming itself to being.
Give boundaries to yourself, O Boundless !

Begrenztes sich opfere Grenzenlosem!
Was Grenzen vermisst, es gründe
In Tiefen sich selber Grenzen;
Es hebe im Strome sich,
Als Welle verfliessend sich halten
Im Werden zum Sein sich gestaltend
Begrenze dich, o Grenzenloses !

PISCES   Feb 19 - Mar 20

In the Lost, may Loss be found,
In the Gain, may Gain be lost !
In the grasped may the grasping seek itself*
and retain itself in the Retained !
Through Becoming, raised to Being;
through Being, interwoven in the Becoming !
The Loss is to be Gain in itself !

Im Verlorenen finde sich Verlust,
Im Gewinn verliere sich Gewinn,
Im Begriffenen suche sich das Greifen
Und erhalte sich im Erhalten.
Durch Werden zum Sein erhoben,
Durch Sein zu dem Werden verwoben,
Der Verlust sei Gewinn für sich !

(*or 'In the Comprehended may the comprehending seek itself')

Commentary

The zodiac can be divided into two sections. As we saw earlier, there are seven influences which have brought about a more refined quality in the human being, and there are five influences which have not yet resulted in a refinement of the human being. The former are called "ascending forces" by Rudolf Steiner, and the latter energies are called "descending forces". The zodiac energies which are 'ascending forces' start with Aries, governing the head, and go down to Libra, which governs the hips. The zodiac energies which are 'descending forces' are from Scorpio to Pisces.

In these twelve verses, this duality is reflected. The first seven verses proceed along in a consistent way, developing and strengthening the qualities of the particular zodiac energy. But with the last five verses, this smooth progression disappears. That is, the verses for Scorpio through to Pisces have a different quality; they lack this consistent unfolding of a dynamic. Instead they are turbulent or even contradictory, for in these five verses a line can be followed by a line which has opposite qualities or which points to opposing challenges. For example, with Scorpio, "*Existence – it consumes being-ness, yet in being-ness, existence is maintained*;" or with Pisces, "*In the Lost, may Loss be found, The Loss is to be Gain in itself!!*"

Contemplating the ego-sense which each of the twelve signs bestow:

ARIES   (Mar 21 - Apr 20)

Arise, O glow of light !	Erstehe, O Lichtesschein,
Grasp Becoming's being,	Erfasse das Werdewesen,
seize the weaving of forces,	Ergreife das Kräfteweben,
shine forth, awakening existence.	Erstrahle dich, Sein-erweckend.
Through resistance, gain;	Am Widerstand gewinne,
in the flow of time, be refined !	Im Zeitenstrom zerrinne.
O shining light, remain !	O Lichteschein, verbleibe !

Overview

The kind of ego or sense of self which a person has who is born in the sign of Aries is characterised by a strong self-awareness, and hence this person has a lot of initiative. The description of the Aries person, and of all the other zodiac types in these verses, is designed to show the essence of this sign, operative in the psychology of that person. We need to note also that if there are other factors in the individual horoscope that weaken or inhibit these qualities, then the core qualities of that sun-sign zodiac may not be very obvious. It will be the task of that person to strive to become what their birth-sign impels them to be.

Physiologically, Aries forces influence our head and especially our forehead, where we experience ideas which we have encountered, or have worked-out, or even received as intuited ideas. So the chief characteristic of the Aries person is experiencing ideas which he or she strongly wants to put into action. But the actual carrying out of ideas demands really seeing and assessing the world around one. So Aries people are quick to assess their sensory impressions, and to perceive how to place their endeavour into the world.

In considering these twelve verses, we shall also be noting at times Rudolf Steiner's lecture of 22nd Jan. 1914, in the cycle called, *Human and Cosmic Thoughts*, where he describes the particular kind of word-view or ideas about life, that each zodiac sign bestows on a person. In eleven instances in this cycle, Rudolf Steiner uses specific technical terms common in philosophy, such as 'monadism' or 'sensualism'. But in his brief explanation of the twelve worldviews, he does not always define these terms in the same way that philosophy does (the difference is noted when it occurs).

He describes the worldview or attitude of mind of an Aries person – if such a person could consciously formulate their philosophic view of life – as 'idealism'. Now, 'idealism' in philosophy means, in brief, a worldview which concludes that everything in creation owes its existence to a mind (whether of a Deity or a human beholder), a mind which has conceived of the thing in question. Rudolf Steiner's explanation of the Aries type in the lecture corresponds generally to this accepted definition, "they regard everything (in the world around them) to be nothing other than a vehicle for ideas (from spirit realms); ideas which permeate the processes underlying cosmos."

In astrological traditions, the Aries person is, as we noted briefly above, an 'ideas person', experiencing their ideas powerfully, and strongly wanting to act on these ideas. This traditional description of the Aries dynamic refers to the personality of an Aries person, whereas Rudolf Steiner in his lecture describes the Aries dynamic with reference to the more philosophical, analytical qualities of the mind. The two descriptions from Rudolf Steiner, one from the lecture about one's philosophy of life, and the other given here in these verses, are closely linked to each other.

Arise, O glow of light !
In this first line, the 'glow of light' appears to represent the self or 'ego' of an Aries person, with her or his inherent radiance. The radiance or brightness comes from the sheer capacity in the Aries sun-sign for ego-endowed initiatives. A particularly powerful Aries child I know, in her infancy and on into the first year of life, was commonly described by intrigued adults, as "somehow very bright" (meaning in the general area of the head). People actually had the impression of an invisible, yet inwardly perceptible, radiant glow around the little child's head.

Grasp Becoming's being,
The verse urges an Aries person to put her or his initiative into the world around them, by really taking hold of the bustling, active world, in which humanity is undergoing its evolving. This ongoing, surging, growing, developing dynamic in our world is here called a "Becoming".

Seize the weaving of forces,
This line urges the Aries person to carry out their core characteristic quality, of actively merging their own will with the complex fabric of people and events in their life, as woven by karma.

shine forth, awakening existence."
By being true to their urge for activity, these alert, pioneering people are described as "awakening existence". This line appears to refer to the world around the Aries person being stirred into a more awakened state, precisely through the effect of his or her strong initiative. But this phrase could also refer to his or her own ego or self-sense becoming more inwardly awakened – the advantage of an Aries incarnation. This dynamic is what underlies the ceaseless 'stage of life' on which we are all players for a time, as Shakespeare declares.

Through resistance, gain;
Aries people gain through the experience of resistance to their initiative, and how they then deal with this interface with other people and how these others express their will. This dynamic is common to Aries people, and is well known to experienced astrologers.

In the second last line, I have a major variation to all translations that I have seen:

in the flow of time, be refined !
It is normally translated as: "in the flow of time, dissolve" (or dwindle or fade away, etc). The word used here, "zerrinne", can certainly mean dissolve. But only if here this word does come from the German verb, 'zerrinnen'. It has always been assumed that this is in fact the verb used here. However, I note that such an interpretation would contradict all the earlier parts of the verse, as well as the final line, and in effect, it takes the Aries person into oblivion. However, this interpretation also moves the verse into an inconsistent, contradictory, turbulent mood. But this mood belongs only to the Descending Signs: to the last five zodiac signs. These facts led me to contemplate the German text further and, there is in fact another rare verb (zerrennen) which can have exactly the same form as the German word 'zerrinnen'. But it means 'to be refined' or 'to be re-moulded', usually referring to metals such as iron, in a sculpting or an industrial process.

It seems to me that this is really the word which Rudolf Steiner is using, as it points to the result of the strong initiative of the Aries person. A lifetime as an Aries person has a strongly re-moulding, refining effect on the ego; this is a direct result of the initiative such people manifest. This effect is however all the stronger because the energies of Aries are intimately connected to iron, which comes from Mars, and Mars is that planet which is 'at home' in the sign of Aries. The initiative of the Aries person is therefore greatly dependent upon the forces from Mars, active in their astral body. My suggestion then echoes the refining and improving effect on a metal such as iron, and Aries people are directly interwoven with the force of Mars, from which iron derives.

O shining light, remain !
This final line echoes the first line, and **consolidates** the line just before it (not contradict it as the usual versions do), urging the Aries person to become a lasting reality, which he or she can be, provided their initiative is true to their karma, and energetically pursued.

                    ****

TAURUS   Apr 21 - May 20

Grow brighter, O radiance of being;	Erhelle dich, Wesensglanz,
dimly feel Becoming's power,	Erfühle die Werdekraft,
weave the thread of life into	Verweben den Lebensfaden
being-imbued world existence,	In Wesendes Weltensein,
in contemplative revelation,	In sinniges Offenbaren,
in radiant awareness of existence.	In leuchtendes Seins-Gewahren.
O radiance of being, appear !	O Wesensglanz, erscheine !

Overview
The kind of ego or sense of self which a person has, who is born in the sign of Taurus is characterised by a phlegmatic, easy-going quality, and hence not by a lot of initiative, as change and making effort, as well as unpredictable situations, are all disliked. The description in this

verse of the Taurus person is designed to show the essence of the mindset of a person born in this sign. (As we noted above, these qualities may not be so obvious if there are other factors in the horoscope that are inhibiting the person from being what their birth-sign impels them to be.)

Physiologically, Taurean forces influence our shoulders and neck, including the throat. We have just mentioned the chief characteristics of the Taurus person; but there is a deeper, less obvious aspect to these. Rudolf Steiner taught that Taurean forces are responsible for the denser material body which we have in this current cosmic age. That is, Taurus is the governing zodiac force for this fourth aeon, the Earth aeon. The influence of Taurus can be reflected in the body as a tendency towards a more substantial body structure, especially around the shoulders and neck.

In the lecture cycle called **Human and Cosmic Thoughts**, Rudolf Steiner describes the worldview or attitude of mind of a Taurean person as 'rationalism' – if such a person could consciously formulate their philosophic view of life. Now, 'rationalism' in philosophy means, an attitude that logical thought or rational thinking alone can obtain a competent knowledge of existence. He gives this term a slightly different nuance to normal philosophical usage; that is, the Taurean regards ideas (logical thinking) as valid, as capable of giving a competent knowledge of existence, but not those ideas which are derived from intuitive-spiritual insights.

Grow brighter, O radiance of being;
The radiance of being, as with Aries, appears to refer to the ego-sense of the person, but here the Taurean has less intensity than the fiery Aries. From its first line onwards, this verse steadily intensifies the admonition to the placid Taurean to have a more tangible self: to make that reflected glow more intense.

dimly feel Becoming's power,
The phlegmatic tendency of the Taurean person can be improved if she or he senses how creation itself is not standing still, but is in a process of Becoming. There are powerful energies underlying this process, and placid Taureans are assisted in engaging their will, if they can sense the power that underlies the ongoing, evolving world.

weave the thread of life into
being-imbued world existence,
The task of the Taurean is to make their will sufficiently empowered so that they do imbue their world with initiative – a world which should be perceived as indeed very real (or 'being-imbued'). In this way, their will-forces become a vibrant part of their karmic reality. Failure to do precisely this is a major problem for Taureans.

in contemplative revelation,
The verse then proceeds to urge the Taurean to unfold their initiative in two ways: one is by contemplative revelation, the other, (in the next line) is by a radiant awareness of existence. With regard to the contemplative revelation, this is connected to another, core dynamic of Taurus: the way that we incarnated people think. With 'rationalism' as their inherent philosophy, the experiencing of one's ideas or thought-life is a natural feature of these people. But Taurus is connected with earth-oriented (non-spiritual) thinking in a potent way. The capacity for normal thinking (which Rudolf Steiner refers to as earth-bound brain consciousness) derives from the ability to form somewhat flat mental images in our mind. This capacity replaces what we have in spiritual realms before being incarnated: namely living astral thought-forms (called 'imaginations' by Rudolf Steiner).

72

Rudolf Steiner taught that this capacity for mental images (from which we can develop concepts) actually comes from Taurus. As people in the latter phase of Lemuria began to develop this type of earthly consciousness, more and more inert mineral substances permeated our tenuous physical body, condensing it and resulting in a hardened, calcium-based skeleton. And this process was sustained by forces from Taurus, which is the primary zodiac force for our current Aeon;

> That which caused the mineral substance (or 'ash') to penetrate into the human body was *the thinking* (the body-bound, conceptual thinking)...and to the same degree that the skeletal system became denser, the human being became permeated by (earthly) thoughts, {and hence} by self-consciousness.[41]

And with regard to the correspondence of zodiac energies to our twelve senses, it is Taurus which is associated with the faculty of thought, to forming earth-based thoughts. So in this line of the verse, the Taurean person is being encouraged to become more contemplative; this is, to develop a more 'imaginative' consciousness. Then *living* thoughts from the spiritual world, (which are reflected in the ether body) can be cognized, and not just earthly mental images. This means in effect to go beyond 'rationalism' and thereby reach to more spiritual views of existence.

in radiant awareness of existence.
This is the second way that the verse is admonishing the Taurean to develop their engagement with the world or their will. Whereas the first way is in effect to 'go within', and experience some intuitive higher ideas, the second way is to 'go without'. For the Taurean needs to direct effort to the world around about them, so that he or she becomes vividly aware of the duties, opportunities and challenges that life is presenting.

O radiance of being, appear !
This last line sums up the general mood of all the preceding lines, urging the Taurean to achieve the initiative and alertness referred to in the verse, and invoked in line one.

****

GEMINI   May 21 - June 21

Disclose yourself, sun-existence,	Erschliesse dich, Sonnesein,
resist the urge to rest,	Bewege den Ruhetrieb,
encompass the desire to strive	Umschliesse die Strebelust
toward mighty prevailing of life,	Zu mächtigem Lebewalten,
toward blissful world-comprehending,	Zu seligem Weltbegreifen,
toward fruitful maturing of Becoming.	Zu fruchtendem Werdereifen.
O sun existence, persist !	O Sonnesein, verharre !

Overview
The kind of ego or sense of self which a person has who is born in the sign of Gemini is characterised by a sanguine quality, where obligations and duties are somewhat resented, but where changing or unpredictable life-situations are welcome. The description in this verse of the Gemini person is designed to show the essence of the attitudes typically found in a person born under this sign. As we noted above, these qualities may not be obvious if there are other factors in the horoscope inhibiting the person from being what their birth-sign impels them to

---

[41] Rudolf Steiner lect. of 16th March 1908, in GA 102, *The Influence of Spiritual Beings on Man.*

be. Physiologically, Gemini forces influence our arms and hands. A prominent quality with Gemini people is the ability to be dexterous and agile, and they are also gifted at assessing a situation, thus responding quickly and ably.

In the *Human and Cosmic Thoughts* lecture cycle, Rudolf Steiner describes the worldview or attitude of mind of a Gemini person (if such a person could consciously formulate their philosophic view of life) as 'mathematic-izing'. Now, 'mathematic-izing' is the one term amongst the twelve given in this lecture-cycle, which has no parallel in philosophy. Rudolf Steiner explains that it means, an attitude which regards as the only valid basis for assessing existence, whatever knowledge that can be expressed in mathematical formulae. What we can say here is that this does have a connection to the non-emotive mental agility and cleverness which is a common feature of Gemini people.

Disclose yourself, sun-existence,
We note that this is the only one of the twelve verses which directly invokes a stronger sun presence. This first line is urging that the sun forces be more manifest, and this suggests that the ego-forces are thereby strengthened. The result is that the sanguine Gemini person can have a more goal-oriented life. The Gemini person needs this help, because he or she can easily retreat from initiative and thus engagement with the earthly reality underlying their life. This problem is pointed out in the humorous satirical version of these verses which Rudolf Steiner gave at the same time as giving the Twelve Moods. The satirical verse for Gemini tells us that this person easily dismisses the earthly reality; "the bright ego feels itself torn away from mere physical thinking and...{going along on an easy, but false path} thereby gets thrown away from ...the path of noble spiritual striving..."

resist the urge to rest,   or *more literally, 'stir up the urge to rest'*
My version seems to be a clearer translation of the German expression, which if translated literally, is '*stir up the urge to rest*'. But a literal version does not work so well in English, suggesting that a person should make even stronger the urge to do nothing. The 'urge to rest' here refers not so much to being lazy, but to the inherent Gemini tendency to avoid duties and burdens, and instead to relax and just cruise through life, which can include a life-style of being quite busy, but not busy in a way that makes real demands on the self. This results in avoiding having genuine initiative, which is a core challenge for Gemini people. This is the result of an urge in the ego, in the core sense-of-self to inwardly rest, to not unfold any real initiative. A strengthened ego-sense overcomes this.

encompass the desire to strive
Again the admonition is for the Gemini person to engage their ego, and thus to put effort – sustained effort – into a worthwhile activity. As the next lines make clear, this call is for the Gemini person to not drift along in an excessively sanguine way.

toward mighty prevailing of life,
This follows on from the earlier line, defining the outcome of inner and also outer effort. The Gemini person should avoid a smooth coasting along way of living, and really ensure that they respond to challenges that they experience.

towards blissful world-comprehending,
Another outcome for this person concerns their mental attitudes. They can comprehend the world, and perhaps quite cleverly, there need not be a superficial gliding along. But the mind is still not being used in a deep way, a way that yields understanding. The German text here can

also be translated as '**towards blessed world-comprehending**'. Whether the outcome is a happy, blissful one or a blessed one, will depend upon the evolvement of the person.

toward fruitful maturing of Becoming.
If the two goals urged in the two preceding lines are attained, then the on-going evolving and inner growth (or Becoming) of the Gemini person will mature in a way which will be fruitful for their spirit.

O sun existence, persist !
The last line then pleads that the ego-sense of this sanguine person be enhanced and endure on for a long time.

                    ****

CANCER   June 22 - July 22

Thou resting luminous glow,	Du ruhender Leuchteglanz,
engender warmth of life,	Erzeuge Lebenswärme,
make warm the life of soul,	Erwärme Seelenleben,
towards empowered proving of self,	Zu kräftigen Selbst-Bewähren,
towards spiritual self-permeating,	Zu geistigen Selbst-Durchdringen,
in a tranquil bringing forth of light.	In ruhigem Licht-Erbringen.
Thou luminous glow, acquire strength !	Du Leuchteglanz, erstarke !

Overview
The kind of ego or sense of self which a person has, who is born in the sign of Cancer, is characterised by a strongly emotional quality. This makes them very vulnerable, as the Cancerian person can so easily feel traumatized when they encounter a lack of love, or harshness. But if the Cancerian person feels loved and at peace, then she or he is especially kind and supportive. Physiologically, Cancer forces govern the chest-cage, which gives protection to the heart; the Cancerian will protect themselves from emotionally difficult situations, by coldly withdrawing into a kind of shell.

Thou resting luminous glow,
engender warmth of life,
Together these two lines inaugurate a quality that permeates the entire verse; the Cancerian person is encouraged to meet their life experiences with a confidence that radiates warmth, instead of retreating into a cold, insecure, defensive attitude.

make warm the life of soul,
Again, encouragement is given to the Cancerian to allow their soul to be warm. That is, to step into life with a positive attitude and confidence, and not to fall prey to the negative Cancerian trait of growing cold and shrinking back into their 'shell', when feeling isolated.

towards empowered proving of self,
This line tells the Cancerian that by taking up the challenge to have the warm, confident attitude urged on them by the earlier lines, they are moving towards a very significant life-goal

for themselves, that of proving that they can face the rigours of life with inner strength. This is a message which is especially relevant to the Cancerian, as they are predisposed to feeling that they are not gifted with inner strength; and so they step sideways around difficult emotional confrontations, imitating the crab.

towards spiritual self-permeating, in a tranquil bringing forth of light.
These two lines point to the deeper challenge for the sensitive, vulnerable Cancerian: to allow a higher quality to predominate, rather than strong emotions, which can easily be self-centred. This suggests that influences from the Spiritual-self should permeate the soul, inaugurating the process of becoming an empowered person, with inner tranquility. This is the opposite dynamic of being self-centred and shielding oneself within a crab-like shell. There is here a subtle link to one aspect of the philosophy of a Cancerian person, as explained in the **Human and Cosmic Thoughts** lecture cycle.[42]

There Rudolf Steiner describes the Cancerian philosophy as 'materialism'. This term is understood in philosophy and by Rudolf Steiner in similar ways, primarily that one considers only matter to be a reality, whilst ideas of spiritual realities are mere theory. But nothing in this verse points to a materialistic type of person, for of course an evolved Cancerian can be a spiritually-minded person. The reason for the differences between what is found in the lecture cycle, and what is given in these verses, is that whereas the lecture cycle is about the twelve different philosophical attitudes, these twelve verses are about the over-all personality produced by your sun-sign. But a comment by Rudolf Steiner in the lecture cycle is relevant here, that the Cancerian person philosophically, "...remains fixed to whatever impression makes the most impact on them..."[43] and naturally, in our modern era, this will be impressions from the material, physical world. Hence philosophically speaking, materialism is near to them.

Looking now at the line, "**towards spiritual self-permeating**", this urges the Cancerian not to be so vulnerable to whatever impression makes the most impact on them. But here it means the soul, particularly the emotions being affected by harsh or unkind emotions from others. If the Cancerian can let a higher, more noble attitude prevail (coming from their Spiritual-self) then they can make real progress in personal development, and integrate the finer Cancerian qualities into their ego. For as we have noted earlier, our ego (our sense of self) is deeply influenced by, or one could say 'permeated by', the zodiac energies of our sun-sign (and the rising sign.)

Thou luminous glow, acquire strength !
The final line sums up all the preceding lines and urges the Cancerian to really be a person of inner strength, and thus no longer be so exposed to the world, so emotionally vulnerable.

****

LEO   July 23 - Aug 23

Pervade with sensory power	Durchströme mit Sinngewalt
what the world's being has become,	Gewordenes Weltensein,
and a muted sensing of being-ness within,	Erfühlende Wesenschaft
towards a willed decision for existence.	Zu wollendem Seinentschluss.
In flowing brightness of life,	In strömenden Lebensschein,
in prevailing pain of becoming,	In waltender Werdepein,
with senses' might, arise !	Mit Sinngewalt, erstehe !

---

[42] This has four lectures given in Berlin, from 20-23rd January 1914 (GA 151).
[43] Ibid, lecture, 22nd Jan. 1914.

Overview

The kind of ego or sense of self which a person has, who is born in the sign of Leo, is characterised by strong awareness of one's physical appearance and social image. In addition, there is an inherent tendency to be in charge of situations, to giving other people suggestions (or orders!) as to what to do. The description in this verse of the Leo person, as with all these verses, is designed to make clear the essence of the attitudes typically found in a person born under this sign. (As we have noted before, these qualities may not be very obvious if there are other factors in the horoscope that are weakening or inhibiting the person from being what their birth-sign impels them to be.) Physiologically, Leo forces influence our heart. A prominent quality with Leo people is the ability to be warm-hearted, and wanting to help others to unfold their initiative, to find a way to be effective in the world. Or the Leo person can be dominating and demanding of others, depending upon the level of evolvement of the soul.

Pervade with sensory power

The first line points to a central dynamic in the Leo person, which is the ability to assess and then respond energetically to what their senses report about their world. This refers especially to opportunities and tasks they can discern as being offered by the world. But furthermore, in the lecture, from *Human and Cosmic Thought*, about the twelve possible philosophical world-views, the Leo person is called a 'sensualist' by Rudolf Steiner. He explains, in harmony with mainstream philosophy, that here this word means a person who regards as sure and valid only that which the senses report, and who therefore feels that whatever the intellect may conclude about the sense-world is not so relevant, and is of little value. So the power that sensory experiences have for the Leo person is especially strong.

what the world's being has become,

The second line, "*what the world's being has become,*" is somewhat different to the wording found in most other translations, which is usually 'matured existence of all worlds'. The word 'mature' is used by Rudolf Steiner in other verses, but here he has chosen to use the German term 'gewordenes', which does not mean 'matured' as such. It means that which has already come into being some time ago and has developed on to become what it is now. The term 'matured' is certainly quite similar to this, yet it is not quite the same. The nuance given here by the choice of this German word, is that the Leo person, vibrant with will, is encountering the world. But the world he or she is encountering has become what it now is, from what it previously was. In this nuance of meaning, there is the suggestion of a past period of time, during which the world evolved further.

This suggests that the future-tending capacity inherent in the will in the Leo (and the will in anyone is always future-tending), is to grapple with what has been brought into being as their present world situation, from 'The Past'. And following on from this nuance is the possibility that 'The Past' alludes to the time when the Leo person was last incarnate (their previous earth life). So this suggests that what may be needed here is to be aware of karma, that is, to strive to sense what is the best course of action to undertake, relative to one's karma.

and a muted sensing of being-ness within,

Here my translation of this line varies very greatly from all other translations I have seen. The reason for this is, that a crucial German word (erfühlen) occurs here; a word which is rarely understood by today's German people, (in anthroposophical circles or otherwise) let alone by English-speaking translators. The texts in which it occurs were printed in the old 'fraktur' or 'Gothic' German, which most German people of today can no longer read. This word had become archaic already around 1900-1910. The largest German-English dictionary from 1901 does not even give an entry for it,[44] whilst modern German dictionaries give only the definition:

---

[44] The huge Muret English-German Dictionary (2,368 Foolscap triple-column pages) simply refers the reader to the associated word, "ertasten" - which means to probe or grope around; a much less comprehensive verb.

'to sense emotionally something'. But the meaning of this word, especially in the works of Rudolf Steiner, actually is: 'to dimly or vaguely sense something (within)'. So crucial is this word in spiritual-psychological knowledge, that Rudolf Steiner used it very, very frequently. It occurs more than 600 times in his Complete Works. The word became prominent in the 18th century, and was used on into the 19th century. For example in the writings of C. M. Wieland (1733-1833):

> „...ſo weit meine fähigkeit das eigenthümliche von Ciceros ſchreibart zu erfühlen reicht.“
> = „...so weit meine Fähigkeit das Eigenthümliche von Ciceros Schreibart zu erfühlen reicht.“ (Wieland's translation of letters of Cicero: 1, XXII.)
> = "...in so far as my ability reaches to *inwardly sense* the characteristic features of the way Cicero writes."

Here the term 'inwardly sense' means to sense or feel something, but only **indistinctly**. Rudolf Steiner uses the word in precisely this way, because it allowed him to contrast a vague sensing (or feeling) in our consciousness to a clear, ego-aware perceiving. See more about this word in the Appendix, p. 96.) Hence with Rudolf Steiner, the faintness or dimness aspect of the word is emphasized. As such it became a key word in his anthroposophical texts and lectures, (although this especial nuance is rarely recognized). It is especially able to illustrate a primary concept in anthroposophy concerning the difference between a consciousness which is not acutely aware, and the spiritually-aware consciousness, especially once spiritual wisdom awakens in a person.

For example he says;

> Auf diesem Punkte wird das *Erfühlen* von wiederholten Erdenleben zu einem wirklichen Erlebnis.   (In GA volume 13, p.320)
> = At this point the *dim inner-sensing* of past lives becomes an actual experience.

Or,

> Wenn wir nach außen schauen, sehen wir das Gelb; wir *erfühlen* daran als Unterton das Anregende, das von außen gewissermaßen aktiv (wird). (In GA volume 73a, p.256; *Fachwissenschaften und Anthroposophie.*)
>
> = When we gaze outwards, we see the colour yellow, and therewith we *faintly sense*, as an undertone, its stimulating aspect, which is active from outside, so to speak.

This word is used in this same way in the Mystery Plays and also in meditative verses. For further examples from Rudolf Steiner, see the Appendix. When this word occurs in these twelve verses, or in other anthroposophical texts, it is usually incorrectly translated. This has lead to such versions of the above line, *and a muted sensing of being-ness within,* as: "Being's feeling entity", or "feeling being's essence" or "Perceptive element of Beings". With these, it is either difficult to discern any real meaning, or the meaning may well be clear, but not at all correct to the meaning of the German text.

This line then, *"and a muted sensing of being-ness within",* is urging the Leo person to 'pervade with senses' might' not only the physical world but also their own, somewhat dim sense of self. Now the outgoing Leo person usually does have an (apparently) strong of sense of self, but this is actually more an **externalized** self-sense. By this I mean a strong astrality, derived from the Leo's considerable power to be active in the world.

This is not necessarily the deeper self-awareness which has a strong inner core, arising from the stronger ego-sense that the spiritual-soul produces. This deeper ego-sense is able to maintain itself strongly in a non-active introspective, meditative state, devoid of sensory impressions. To over-simplify the situation, one could say that this deeper sense of self is usually easier for a more inward, contemplative type of person to attain, rather than the extraverted, action-oriented Leo.

towards a willed decision for existence.
The preceding lines culminate here, with this admonition to have conscious determination to put one's will into one's life. There is the subtle nuance, that 'the will' meant here, goes beyond the personal will, and reaches up to the will or intentions that live within a deeper level of the soul-life, namely the spiritual-soul, where our intuitive awareness lies. This level can start to be attained by the Leo when he or she deepens their sense of self.

In flowing brightness of life,
It is a core feature of the Leo person, when they are manifesting their initiative that, subtly observed, they seem to radiate a brightness. The sun is especially empowered in Leo (it is 'domiciled' in this sign) and, just as the planets only shine because the sun shines on them, the Leo person seeks to empower other people to shine, through manifesting their abilities with initiative – but sparked off by encouragement from the Leo person.

in prevailing pain of becoming,
When any initiative is underway, there will be times of stress and difficulty. But when a Leo person is involved in initiatives, this usually involves him or her actively encouraging, or even being in charge of, other people, on behalf of a project, and this brings significant challenges. Their active participation in the ongoing evolving of creation (or its 'Becoming') does involve pain and stress.

with senses' might, arise !
As with all the verses, the last line echoes the first line, and here the first line, which encourages a pervading of life with the senses' power, is brought to the natural conclusion of the person's ego coming strongly into being (arising) through engaging with, and responding to one's sensory experiences.

****

VIRGO   Aug 24 - Sept 23

Behold the realms, O soul !	Die Welten erschaue, Seele !
May the soul take hold of realms –	Die Seele ergreife Welten,
may the mind comprehend being,	Der Geist erfasse Wesen,
from powers-of-life be efficacious,	Aus Lebensgewalten, wirke,
through experience of the Will, build,	Im Willenserleben baue !
trust in the blossoming of the cosmos.	Dem Weltenerblüh'n vertraue !
O soul - cognize the beings !	O Seele, erkenne die Wesen !

Overview
The kind of ego or sense of self which a person has, who is born in the sign of Virgo, is characterised by strong awareness of tidiness, orderliness and of being averse to behaviour which is considered to be inappropriate. There is as well a capacity to analyse a situation clearly, and at times to be pedantic. Physiologically, Virgo forces influence the stomach. The description in this verse of the Virgo person, (as with all these verses), is designed to clearly characterize the dynamics typically found in a person born under this sign, without mixing in influences from other features in the horoscope.

In the lecture cycle about the twelve possible world-views, *Human and Cosmic Thought*, the Virgo person is called a 'phenomenalist' by Rudolf Steiner. He explains, in harmony with mainstream philosophy, that this term means a person who is quite grounded, in that he or she works with the physical world, as a reality which the senses reveal; yet is someone who does not regard the sense-world as necessarily a true reality, which could have an objective existence, if **we** did not in fact exist. We see how there is an improvement here philosophically, over Leo, in that the material world is no longer considered as the only realm which we can regard as real; human beings and their sensing capacity are needed too. (As we progress through the zodiac signs in terms of a philosophical world-view, the signs become increasingly less materially oriented.)

Behold the realms, O soul !

The inner need for the Virgoan is, in the first instance, to really perceive all the realms (or 'worlds') which make up our earthly world which they are seeing (and hearing, touching, etc). The tendency towards an inner rigidity or pedantry in Virgoans can act as a barrier, preventing them from really discerning all that is in the world. Secondly, on a more spiritual level, this line is admonishing the earthy Virgoan to be open in heart and mind to the reality of the spiritual worlds. We saw how in the Stuttgart zodiac, in the new image for Virgo, the kind of consciousness which is open to the living cosmos is indicated. This shows a feminine figure (the emerging Spirit-self) surrounded by an outline of the entire twelve-fold cosmos. This image suggests that the Virgoan can be sensitive to the spiritual forces flowing from spiritual realms, and thus to the spiritual reality underlying the zodiac in general (that is, from the Logos).

May the soul take hold of realms –

This line is urging the Virgoan not to allow a too orderly, nor a too critical, attitude to block him or her from fully discerning, and then participating in, all the realms whose influences underlie the human existence, and which include those which are 'behind' the zodiac energies.

may the mind comprehend being,

This line complements the earlier one, urging the Virgoan to indeed expand beyond a too structured, a too dogmatic view of existence and achieve a comprehension of the fullness of life. Most translations have here, *may the spirit comprehend being;* but here, and often elsewhere, the German word "Geist" is incorrectly understood to mean 'spirit'. For Rudolf Steiner can use this word to mean either 'intelligence' or 'spirit', that is, a specifically 'Devachanic' reality, a spiritual reality. So the reader has to determine which meaning he intends. This is because this word has both of these meanings, amongst several other meanings; but a major one is simply the intelligence or mind of a person.

Here a Virgoan's 'spirit' cannot be referred to, because the 'spirit', in the true deeper sense of the Spirit-self, is rarely present, in any strong way, in people, other than initiates. And also the human spirit (the Spirit-Self) has an inherent ability to "comprehend being", it doesn't need to be urged to achieve this. It is also true that sometimes the mind of the human being is referred to as 'spirit' by Rudolf Steiner. This is because in German there is an old and noble tradition that the human intelligence derives from a spiritual realm, beyond the astral plane.

from powers-of-life be efficacious,

This line is urging the Virgoan to exert an active influence in their world, that is, to have efficacy and thereby achieve their goals, by drawing on those life-energies which are available to a person in the physical world. For this to happen, the Virgoan would have to step fully into

80

what earthly life offers, and overcome any feeling of remaining separate from many aspects of life.

through experience of the Will, build,
The admonition here is a natural extension of the preceding line, because it is through exerting one's will that a person can be in a position to build. That is, to bring new impulses into the world, incorporating new dynamics into creation.

trust in the blossoming of the cosmos.
This admonition represents a particularly hard challenge for the Virgoan. For a person with this sun-sign to have trust in the cosmos blossoming, goes directly against their cautious and prudent nature. That is, to trust that the world shall respond in a positive and bountiful way to what he or she is attempting to achieve, and to relax their urge to control and manage everything, is really difficult. It is much easier for the polar opposite zodiacal sun-sign, the Piscean person, to do this. (This line can also be translated in the plural: *trust in the blossoming of worlds, or realms.*)

O soul – cognize the beings !
This final line sums up the over-all urging to the Virgoan to step beyond the discreet veil which they cautiously place between themselves and the world, and to really sense the cosmos around them, with all of its beings. On a higher level, with regard to the philosophical feature of Virgoans, who are, as we noted above, 'phenomenalists', this line could be seen as a call to become spiritually perceptive. That is, to overcome the hesitant 'phenomenalist' attitude and to acknowledge the existence of spiritual beings and spiritual reality.

****

LIBRA   Sept 24 - Nov 22

The realms maintain realms,	Die Welten erhalten Welten,
In being, being-ness is experienced,	Im Wesen, erlebt sich Wesen,
In existence, existence is encompassed,	Im Sein umschliesst sich Sein
and being-ness makes operative being-ness	Und Wesen erwirket Wesen
for an ongoing pouring-forth of deeds,	Zu werdendem Tatergiessen,
in tranquil world enjoyment.	In ruhendem Weltgeniessen.
O realms, uphold realms !	O Welten, ertraget Welten !

Overview
Before we consider the important features of the Libran person, we need to note that the lines 2 and 3 are subtle, and grammatically can be translated in several ways. They can be as given above:

> In being, being-ness is experienced,
> In existence, existence is encompassed,

But line One could be: "In being, being is experienced"; there is very little difference between these two. I have used 'being-ness' to clarify what I understand line One to mean. This word does make the meaning clearer, but the German language doesn't really have any specific word for this strained word, 'being-ness'. But lines One and Two could be reflexive, that is:

being experiences itself in being,
In existence, existence encompasses itself,

This alternative version, of having the reflexive version seems incorrect to what Rudolf Steiner means here, because the verse is about how the Libran person experiences their life, not about how 'being' or 'existence' (thought of philosophical realities) experience themselves, so to speak; since these are abstract ideas, but these verses are about people.

We shall explore these lines below. The kind of ego or sense of self which a person has who is born in the sign of Libra, is delightfully sociable, sensitive and often artistic. But the Libran ego-sense is not strong, so he or she easily defers to others. Librans also have difficulty in being decisive, especially if two other people each give conflicting advice. The Libran is hesitant to state what his or her views and wants are, if there is a chance of anger or social disharmony arising from doing this. So engagement with the more demanding aspects of the world is not easy for Librans. This verse focuses on the main dynamics of a person born under this sign.

The realms maintain realms,

This first line can also be translated as 'The realms (or worlds) *sustain* realms (or worlds)'. In fact, whichever nuance of meaning you take, the meaning of this line is veiled. It appears to indicate that, throughout creation the various realms or worlds are interlinked, sustaining or supporting each other. This could be seen as suggesting to the Libran how unwise it is, through lack of ego-strength, to remain only on the periphery of one's world, with its people, challenges and opportunities, a world which their karma has brought about.

In being, being-ness is experienced,

Following on from the first line, this line is pointing out that if one is actually incarnate, that is, 'in a physical state of being', then this state of being is what you are now meant to be experiencing. You therefore should make the effort to be fully within the state of being of someone incarnate on the Earth.

In existing, existence is encompassed,

This third line follows on from the second, pointing out that in the state of existing, or having physical existence, existence itself is actually being taken on; it is being embraced or encompassed. This dynamic should be recognized, and the hesitant, self-effacing Libran tendency rejected.

and being-ness makes operative being-ness,

Here the consequences of the earlier lines are pointed out: consequences which the Libran person needs to contemplate. The message in this line is quite difficult to grasp. It is stating that in the physical world (or 'existence') the condition of having tangible, real being (or being-ness) results in this same condition of really existing, becoming operative in the Libran person. That is, she or he is then taking on more reality, or more 'being'. It is all about actually allowing the ego, the self, to really manifest.

for an ongoing pouring-forth of deeds,

Here we encounter the outcome of the earlier exhortations for the Libran to be someone who is an achiever, someone in whose deeds the ego has placed its imprint. The Libran is able to exert their initiative, but they have to find the ego-strength to really do this. Their capacity to accomplish goals is indicated in the lecture from *Human and Cosmic Thoughts*, where these people are defined as 'realists'. But here Rudolf Steiner is using this term in a manner quite different to mainstream philosophy.

He explains that a 'realist' is someone who is able to see clearly and deeply into whatever they are interested in, "...they are able to feel and experience very sensitively whatever is around about them..." This acute perceptivity can merge with the Libran refined sense of aesthetics, to bring about a worthwhile, impressive result. However, we should not expect the Libran to unfold initiative of a highly competitive or forceful kind to have the pleasure of becoming the assertive, fiery victor, ready to take on ever more challenges.

in tranquil world enjoyment.
This final line points to an unusual conclusion with regard to initiative for the Libran; it is to enter the state of tranquility, where he or she can enjoy the results of their deeds. This outcome closely echoes the desired outcome in personal development for the Libran in that other set of sun-sign meditations, *the Twelve Virtues*. One finds there for Libra the meditative words, "Contentment becomes tranquillity" (in German, Zufriedenheit wird zu Gelassenheit). But this real contentment only arises if the Libran is true to themselves, and not a tool or mirror of someone else. Such a social dynamic breeds inner discontent; a deeply irritated, uneasy mood can become a Libran reality, exacerbated by the harshness of the world. But once the Libran is true to themselves, then an inner tranquility is possible.

O realms, uphold realms !
The final line invokes a positive outcome for the Libran finding their own initiative. This takes the first line, *The realms maintain realms*, to the higher state, wherein the many interdependent life-waves and realms in creation are upholding or bearing along each other.

****

SCORPIO   Oct 24 - Nov 22

Existence – it consumes being-ness,	Das Sein, es verzehrt das Wesen,
yet in being-ness, existence is maintained.	Im Wesen doch hält sich Sein.
In efficaciousness Becoming disappears,	Im Wirken entschwindet Werden,
in Becoming, efficacy abides.	Im Werden, verharret Wirken.
In chastising cosmic prevailing,	In strafendem Weltenwalten
in punishing self-forming,	In ahndenden Selbst-Gestalten
being-ness maintains the beings.	Das Wesen erhält die Wesen.

Overview
As we noted earlier, Rudolf Steiner's teachings concerning the past history of the Earth provides a new perspective on the complex dynamics of some of the sun-signs, including the Scorpio person. We noted earlier, that some millions of years ago, the sun shone down upon the Earth from the region of Scorpio repeatedly over long ages, humanity changed from primitive, mono-sexed creatures into the two sexes of today. This process eventually enabled the development of a personal individualized intelligence, and also sensual desires. In Chapter 1 we saw that the after-effect of this momentous change in humanity's evolving is reflected in the more intense inner awareness of life's experiences, and included in this are more intense yearnings, thoughts

and desires. In his work with eurythmists, Rudolf Steiner described this characteristic of Scorpio saying "*it is the impulses of stimulation – thinking*".[45]

In the lecture from *Human and Cosmic Thoughts*, Rudolf Steiner identifies the Scorpio's natural philosophy as "dynamism", and he defines this in general accordance with the various mainstream philosophical usages of this term. He states that it is a viewpoint which concludes that behind natural phenomena there exist (invisible) forces, such as gravity, which have a major role in what we see as nature phenomena. So in any given material process, a Scorpio person focuses more on such forces than on matter. Also with Scorpio, we begin with the first of the five turbulent "descending" zodiacal signs.

We remind ourselves here that 'efficacy' and 'efficaciousness' mean 'an active influence', or to bring about an active influence, on something (not simply to work or to be active). These words (and also the word 'operative') translate the German words used here with more nuance, giving a more subtle understanding of the verse.

Existence – it consumes being-ness, (*or, Existence – it consumes {the} being,*)
The first line contains a direct allusion to the inherent nature of the Scorpio person's inner nature, whose soul-processes, whether as yearnings or sensuality or as intense, private thoughts, consume their etheric energies, or subject his or her astral energies to turmoil. Hence to the Scorpio person, it can seem as if their own existence is burning up their soul, so potent is the impact on themselves of their inner life. It is also an esoteric truth that sensuality causes the consuming of life-forces which could otherwise be conserved and spiritualized, providing a basis for higher insights and a more empowered creativity.

Medical science is aware that various physical and mental activities we undertake, cause cells of the body to be used or die. In the anthroposophical view of the world, the mind, or intelligence of the human being, in generating its individual thoughts, causes cells in the body to die off.[46] It was during the old Scorpio Age, when the life-forces were split in two, to allow the creation of the brain, that the development of individual thinking was made possible.

yet in being-ness, existence is maintained.
With this line, we encounter the stark contradictions or polarity dynamics that the turbulent, descending astral energies bring about in a Scorpio person's soul-life. The Scorpio person's life-forces and astrality are not extinguished by their intense inner life. The etheric and astral energies of the Scorpio do not vanish, for these forces are replenished and the person's existence continues on.

In efficaciousness Becoming disappears,
In this line another stark contradictory or polarity dynamic begins to be indicated. In the process of a Scorpio person having an active impact on their life and general environs, (that is, being efficacious), he or she is no longer in the phase of 'becoming'. For they have arrived at the point where they can start to exert an impact on the environs; they are being efficacious.

in Becoming, efficacy abides.
But, following from the above line, the polarity to this is now shown: it is also true that when a person is in the process of inner growth and development (or 'becoming'), then actually, from

---

[45] GA 279, lecture 7th July 1924.
[46] References to this are found in many lectures; e.g., in GA 72 p. 372, GA 209 p. 130, GA 67, p.339, GA 179, p.123, GA 204, p.40

somewhere deep within their soul-life, an influence is being actively exerted (is having efficacy). If this were not so, then the Scorpio person could never be in the process of developing (or 'becoming') because any on-going developing or growing process has to be the result of influences, exerted by some force. So in these two lines, there is a turbulent process of moving between actively exerting one's energy, which influences one's environs, or holding back and engaging with 'becoming'; that is, with the drive to 'come into being' and thus further consolidate oneself.

These two opposite dynamics express the essence of the inner life of the Scorpio person: does he or she feel that they have a clear and stable platform from which to speak their mind, and have some impact (exert an influence) in their social reality? Or does this person feel that they are still 'becoming' and therefore need to refrain from actively having any influence in their social reality? That is, do they still need to be more sure of their own attitudes and their feelings, but especially of other people's response to their possible contribution?

It is not a matter of inner stillness and rest if the Scorpio remains discreet or withdrawn; there is an intense, but private, process going on. The power of this polarity dynamic is considerable, as evidenced by Scorpio being the only zodiacal sign which has two, very different and polar opposite symbols: the furtive, concealed scorpion and the confident, openly displayed eagle.

In chastising cosmic prevailing,

The intensity of the Scorpio's inner life, and their wrestling with the burning challenge of passion, cause a substantial interface with the karma laws or inherent dynamics which govern humanity, especially in regard to the astral realm. In other words, a "cosmic chastising" of the soul can be invoked by the wrong use of life-forces, or by a very turbulent immersion in desires; these are factors associated with life as a Scorpio people. This can be glimpsed if one is familiar with the private inner life and dreams of a Scorpio person; but the insightful astrologer can also see this clearly in retrospect.

One bears in mind here that Rudolf Steiner taught that the moon brings us down to birth, with our karma from the previous life: he calls it the "gate of the Moon".[47] This allows us to conclude that the zodiacal position of the south lunar node[48] reveals our past zodiac influence, that is, what was our past life's main zodiac influence. The reason for this, as explained in *the Horoscope Handbook - a Rudolf Steiner Approach*, is that the most prominent and often the more negative personality qualities of the sign this node is placed in, exist in the person's soul, (in their subconscious).

So if this node is in Scorpio, then in his or her last life, this person had Scorpio as a sun-sign (or as a rising sign). And with these people, one often finds, for example Mars is square to Neptune, and the title for this is, "*the driving force is obscured by unwholesome influences*",[49] which means in effect, that the sexual drive needs to be refined. So before this person is re-born, the hierarchies in their 'chastising cosmic' power arranged this quality which the horoscope reveals.

in punishing self-forming,

The message in this line, can also be seen in retrospect, in the horoscope, showing the wisdom of a spiritual astrology deepened through anthroposophy. Where the south lunar node is in Scorpio, we often find for example amongst the planets, that Venus can be square to Pluto: the title for this is, "*ego-centric emotions which seek aggressive interaction*", which means, amongst

---

[47] Rudolf Steiner, Lect. in Den Hague, 5th Nov. 1922 (GA 218).
[48] The south lunar node is the name for that point in the heavens where the moon's pathway, as it crosses the equator and heads south, intersects with the Earth's equator, (visualized as extended out into space.)
[49] See my, *The Horoscope Handbook - a Rudolf Steiner Approach*.

other problems, that a self-destructive tendency manifests in relationships. Or if Saturn, with negative influences from other planets, is located in House 8, this brings about anxiety concerning death as a child, and also problems in maintaining intimate relationships.

And in addition, the Scorpio south lunar node itself, bearing as it does the worst of the previous Scorpio forces, could be located in House 8. This often causes potent problems with passions and relationships, together with an undertone of feeling somehow pursued and punished by life itself. As one commentator wrote "...he feels that he must constantly escape from punishment..."[50] The Scorpio person, in spiritual worlds after death where one merges with the Higher-self, has made the resolution to receive the punishment decreed by karmic-guiding powers, and in this process the soul moulds itself into a higher state of evolvement.

being-ness maintains the beings. (or *being maintains the beings.*)
This line refers back to the two earlier lines, but also back to the first line which declares that "*Existence – it consumes being-ness*". However, this final line makes a positive affirmation that the internalized, fiery Scorpio dynamic does not wither away the Scorpio person, nor any other beings associated with them (physical or spiritual entities) because creation or 'being-ness' is so ordered that it has the capacity within itself to ensure that life continues on. (It seems to me if one translates this line as, *being maintains the beings"* there is no difference to the meaning.)[51]

****

SAGITTARIUS   Nov 23 - Dec 21

Becoming attains the might of being,
into the Existing, Becoming's might dies away.
The Attained concludes striving's desire,
within the prevailing will-power of life.
In dying away, the cosmos' Prevailing matures from within,
forms disappear in forms.
The Existing – feel the Existing !

Das Werden erreicht das Seinsgewalt,
Im Seienden erstirbt die Werdemacht.
Erreichtes beschliesst die Strebelust
In waltender Lebenswillenskraft.
Im Sterben erreift das Weltenwalten,

Gestalten verschwinden in Gestalten.
Das Seiende fühle das Seiende !

Overview
As we noted earlier, Rudolf Steiner's teachings concerning the past history of the Earth provide a new perspective into the complex dynamics of some of the sun-signs, including the Sagittarian person. As we saw in Chapter 1, some millions of years ago the sun shone down upon the Earth from the region of Sagittarius for long ages, when the primordial, turbulent conditions were still presenting a strong challenge to human beings to come into life on Earth. The human being had to exert considerable force to penetrate this foreign environment. As we noted earlier, an after-echo of this challenge is that Sagittarians today are drawn to challenges which demand a lot of them, and which are always giving new possibilities for initiative. In his work with eurythmists, Rudolf Steiner described the characteristic of the Sagittarian person

---

[50] Martin Schulman, "South node in house 8", in *The moon's nodes and reincarnation*, Weiser, New York, 1975.
[51] But if one translates it as *The being maintains the beings*, then this requires one to seek out a particular spiritual entity who does this maintaining; yet no trace of any such entity is indicated in the verse. So I view the word *'the'* here as a requirement of German grammar, which should not be carried over into English, exactly as with this same word in line one.

saying "it is the impulse of the soul who is having an effect on their world through their actions (i.e., being efficacious)".

Becoming attains the might of being,

This line focuses on a dynamic which is one step further ahead of Scorpio. In Scorpio the struggle was about whether to step out and make one's inner life something that impacted on the world around one, but with Sagittarians, there is no such hesitation; they are ready and eager to do something. So the process of coming into being and developing on ('becoming') has been completed and has progressed into really being present in the world.

into the Existing, Becoming's might dies away.

Here the contemplative message of the first line comes to completion; the process of coming into being, of generally developing, is over; so it fades away. But we also have in this line the verb 'to die away' (ersterben), which is often assumed in translations to mean simply 'to die' (sterben), and then the conclusion is drawn that it means death as a major dynamic throughout the cosmos. But the special verb used by Rudolf Steiner here means a fading out, not a (fairly sudden, normal) death. In particular, it also often means a <u>figurative</u> dying away of something, not necessarily a death of a living being.

The Attained concludes striving's desire,

Once the Sagittarian has successfully brought about the completion of their initiative, a sense of fulfillment is their reward, and consequently the desire to strive and work towards the goal comes to an end. But the Sagittarian person strongly faces the world, always seeking actively for a goal that they can undertake, preferably one that challenges them substantially. The human being takes over the reins of their soul's chariot, as it were, and stands strongly in existence. (The translation, "Achievement *brings to a peak* striving's zest" does not seem to give the right nuance for the verb used here, beschließen, to conclude).

within the prevailing will-power of life.

There remains the strong will to be active. For the Sagittarian has an urge to seek out another challenge to satisfy his or her strong urge to put their initiative into the world. Forces from Sagittarius govern the upper legs, by which we move our body through the world. The fiery Sagittarian ego-sense is firmly knitted to what life in the physical world can offer, when in the limbs there pulses the urge to action.

In dying away, the cosmos' Prevailing matures from within,

In this line we encounter a special form of the verb 'to ripen' or 'to mature' (reifen). Only here, and in two other times in the 350 volumes of his Complete Works does Rudolf Steiner use it, in the form 'erreift'. In every other instance (some 54 times) he used the normal form, 'reift'.[52] The difference that this nuance brings to this verb is that, the maturing (or ripening process) occurs specifically through a definite intention from within. So here, the cosmos' activity ripens by its own specific intention, through its own effort. So what has 'died away' or faded out here, and what does this mean for the Sagittarian ? The implication in this line is that there **passes over to the Sagittarian person** an inherent capacity for initiative.

----
52 The two other times are in GA vol. 199 p.227 & GA 157a, p.118.

As we saw in the earlier lines, there is the firstly the "dying away" of "*becoming's might*" as the Sagittarian brings their will into the world. So this person is no longer just in the process of developing and maturing. Secondly, we also saw above, '*The Attained concludes striving's desire*' – meaning that the desire to strive towards a goal is brought to an end as the goal is reached and it dies away too.

So this line speaks of the fading away of "*striving's desire*" as the Sagittarian attains their goal; but it also may refer back to the dying away of "*Becoming's might*", as the Sagittarian is someone who stands strongly in their existing reality. Through these two dying-away processes the "*cosmos' Prevailing matures from within*". In other words, then the cosmic energies emerge in the Sagittarian as an empowered ego-sense and a capacity for initiative. There is an allusion here to the stirring into semi-wakefulness of divine forces, slumbering in the human being.

forms disappear in forms.
A way to approach this otherwise enigmatic line is to merge Rudolf Steiner's teachings about the nature of Devachan with astrological insight into the Sagittarian personality.[53] We have noted how the Sagittarian is drawn to action, but actually with this sun-sign, the idea or concept behind the planned action is just as important as the activity itself. Sagittarians are well known for their predisposition to put into action challenging ideas, or grand concepts. This quality is strengthened by the inherent affinity of Jupiter to this zodiac sign, as Jupiter inspires not only logical thinking, but also intuitive ideas. These ideas have their existence in Devachan, where ideas exist as spiritual forms. Rudolf Steiner taught that the initiate sees these thought-forms in Devachan "...one sees how one form develops into existence by metamorphosis from another form....how forms {disappear and} transform into each other.."[54]

The Existing – feel the Existing !
The meditation ends with the last line echoing the first line – as in all the verses – and bringing to completion the message presented throughout the verse. The first line proclaimed that the process of becoming has definitely merged into the state of fully existing. Thus the last line brings the command that the Sagittarian really senses (or feels) this state, and acts accordingly.

****

CAPRICORN   Dec 22 - Jan 19

May what is in the future rest upon what has been !	Das Künftige ruhe auf Vergangenem
May what has been, dimly sense what is in the future	Vergangenes erfühle Künftiges
for a robust present existence.	Zu kräftigem Gegenwartsein.
In inner life-resistance	Im inneren Lebenswiderstand
may cosmic-being's vigil grow strong,	Erstarke die Weltenwesenswacht,
may life's power to have efficacy blossom.	Erblühe die Lebenswirkensmacht.
What has been – *endure* what is in the future !	Vergangenes ertrage Künftiges !

Overview
With Capricorn as the sun-sign, the personality is strongly self-aware, and consciously forms goals in life. The Capricorn person has a capacity to formulate goals which may be many years ahead. These people also have an unequalled capacity for endurance, for persistence in striving

---

53 It has no link to the odd theory of "a Jupiter law that governs the sacrificing of centaurs" (proposed by W. Erasmy).
54 See "Two Gems from Rudolf Steiner" two lectures from 1904/05 restored, edited and translated by A. Anderson.

towards that goal. The planet Saturn is 'domiciled in' (i.e., naturally in resonance with) Capricorn, and this reinforces the acute sense of having a task to achieve. But Saturn's forces also reinforce the severity of life for these people. It inhibits the chances of early success, and reduces the inclination to be indulgent and to take it easy on oneself.

May what is in the future rest upon what has been !
It is well-known that the key to understanding one's current times is to have a knowledge of history, as the forces responsible for much that happens now, is revealed if one learns about what happened in the past. In a similar way, a core feature of Capricorn people is the sense of how their present shall soon become their past, and that it is upon precisely this time sequence that their future depends.

May what has been, dimly sense what is in the future
This line presents the very essence of the core dynamic of the Capricorn person; they scrutinize the past, even if subconsciously, to see, in retrospect if the past has provided the basis for their future goals. And if in later years, the previously future goals have not now in fact been achieved, then they scrutinize past events, seeking an explanation for this.

for a robust present existence.
This concern about the past, whilst focussed on the future, deprives the Capricorn of many of the benefits and enjoyments of living in the present. Theirs is often a robust, demanding life, bringing difficulties and responsibilities.

In inner life-resistance
This line presents another core dynamic of the Capricorn sun-sign; the feeling that potent resistance to them, to their rightful life-goals and important needs, is being specifically meted out either by people or Providence (that is, karma). It can be translated as 'inner life-withstanding' or 'inner life-opposing'; meaning that in their inner being, the Capricorn person has to do battle with the demands of life. Saturnine energies can bring severe testing into the Capricorn person's pathway, either from other people or from within their own soul-life.

may cosmic-being's vigil grow strong,
This line, and the following line, offer a profound contemplation on the purpose behind the discipline, severity and possible harshness of the Capricorn life. Here the hope is about the effect of their challenges and restrictions, of their struggle towards an empowered ego-hood. The plea is for the monitoring, sustaining and guiding activity of divine beings in the cosmos, which underlie the Capricorn's consciousness, to become more effective; and perhaps also to become more discernible to the person.

may life's power to have efficacy blossom.
This line completes the contemplation on the purpose behind the severity and possible harshness of the Capricorn life. The hope is that the Capricorn person gains an increased capacity to actively make an impact, to have a real influence, in the world; and not to stay quietly in the background, avoiding any opportunities to become prominent, as people of this sun-sign are prone to do. But if the Capricorn can achieve an increased capacity to make a contribution to life, it usually manifests later in their life.

What has been – endure what is in the future !
This final line declares a positive outcome to the primary need and yearning of Capricorn people. Their future goals can succeed because their previous strivings have laid a solid foundation for the challenges in this current life.

****

AQUARIUS Jan 20 - Feb 18

May the confined surrender to the boundless !	Begrenztes sich opfere Grenzenlosem.
What feels the lack of boundaries, may it establish	Was Grenzen vermisst, es gründe
in depths boundaries for itself.	In Tiefen sich selber Grenzen;
May it raise itself in the stream,	Es hebe im Strome sich,
as a wave flowing away, retaining itself,	Als Welle verfliessend sich halten
In the Becoming forming itself to being.	Im Werden zum Sein sich gestaltend
Give boundaries to yourself, O Boundless !	Begrenze dich, o Grenzenloses !

Overview
We saw in Chapter 1 that the Stuttgart image for Aquarius derives from the dynamics that humanity encountered in the Hyperborean Age. The contemplation in this verse of the Aquarian personality is referring to the dynamics prevailing back then. As we noted earlier, the Earth was then a watery, airy planet with powerful ethereal energies weaving through it. Humanity existed in a very primitive ethereal, aquatic type of body, which dissolved and re-formed. Here we shall consider some more revelations from Rudolf Steiner, from unpublished archive notes. These concern the Aquarian phase of the Hyperborean Age, and his comments are crucial to understanding this verse,

> "When the human being swims around about in such a fluidic {and dark} environment, and they themselves {their body} are also of a fluidic nature, then it was the case with these human beings, that they would not perceive the boundaries between themselves and other human beings. One first perceives boundaries only when things become visible. Also the {primordial} separate human being did not differentiate itself so sharply from other human beings; it felt itself more as part of the general environs….an object is only then outside us when we see its boundaries outside of us."[55]

This tenuous body gave human beings a specific place in which to exist, but the feeling of having no perimeter or boundary was a prominent experience, a problem which was intensified by the restless metamorphosing of their environment. Human beings had to struggle with this constantly metamorphosing, restless watery environment. Medically, Aquarians today often reflect this ancient dynamic, having problems in the circulatory system, as their blood stream has trouble flowing out to the boundaries of the body, causing coldness in the extremities.

May the confined surrender to the boundless.
An inherent and central urge in the Aquarian person, which helps them to maintain their inner peace, is to seek freedom whenever they feel confined or 'bounded'. This sense of not being free, of being enclosed, occurs also when they are having to acquiesce to, or act upon, ideas that they do not agree with. If they repress this urge to be free because of social pressures, they can

---

[55] Archive manuscript of April 1904, notes of lecture taken by F. Seiler.

easily become unwell. The Aquarian person is very much the 'free-spirit'. They are the most individualistic people of all the zodiac signs.

What feels the lack of boundaries, may it establish

Despite the strong inner need for freedom on various levels, there is also an awareness of the need for some boundaries. If the Aquarian fails to create these, an ungrounded type of irresponsible 'freedom' ensnares them (whereas in old Hyperborea, they would have merged into their environs).

in depths boundaries for itself.

This line completes the above thought, that the Aquarian nevertheless has to establish limits to her or his individualism with its strong urge for intellectual and emotional freedom. They need to decide upon some definite, even if discreet, boundaries, if their personal and professional life is to prosper.

May it raise itself in the stream,

The next two lines, in describing the inner life of the Aquarian person today, use the central dynamic of the old Hyperborean Age. In the image from the Stuttgart building and the 1912/13 Calendar, we see the human being precariously trying to exist in its turbulent fluidic environment. Likewise the Aquarian today has to assert its individual nature, but.....

as a wave flowing away, retaining itself,

.... it must also achieve what the second line is presenting in a powerful, contradictory image. The wave has to merge into the turbulent sea, yet at the same time, this wave has to retain its own separate reality. Obviously for a wave to do this is impossible. But the Aquarian personality will always want to express their individuality, yet they must be part of a fully genuine social interaction, whilst maintaining their own nature.

We note here that translations with "sustaining itself" don't quite present the full nature of the imagery; it is not so much about 'sustaining' as retaining one's separate self-hood. We can note here that when a wave 'flows away', it actually merges back into the sea, and this is exactly what the dynamic here is about, and this is what the Stuttgart image indicates.

In the Becoming forming itself to being.

In the difficult process of constantly finding and maintaining their own needs and goals within their many social interactions, the Aquarian person forms his or her actual personality. In the process of a continuous ongoing consolidating ('becoming') of their reality, is where this person enters into the state of actually being himself or herself.

Give boundaries to yourself, O Boundless !

As with all these verses, the last line then rounds off the dynamic which the first line declares. Here in this zodiac sign, which is part of the turbulent 'descending' zodiacal energies, the last line reverses what the first line urges. It is not urging that the Aquarian person, when feeling confined, surrender to a boundless or freer reality, but rather that this person, when feeling somewhat lacking in regard to the boundaries, gives boundaries to oneself. That is, the deep urge in this sun-sign for unbounded, sanguine ways of living, is to be reined in enough for them to see where, socially, boundaries are needed.

****

PISCES   Feb 19 - Mar 20

In the Lost, may Loss be found,	Im Verlorenen finde sich Verlust,
In the Gain, may Gain be lost !	Im Gewinn verliere sich Gewinn,
In the grasped, may the grasping be sought	Im Begriffenen suche sich das Greifen
and retain itself in the Retained !	Und erhalte sich im Erhalten.
Through Becoming, raised to Being;	Durch Werden zum Sein erhoben,
through Being, interwoven in the Becoming !	Durch Sein zu dem Werden verwoben,
The Loss is to be Gain in itself !	Der Verlust sei Gewinn für sich !

Overview

The Piscean person is very sociable and empathetic, often psychic, and can generously use their insights and compassion to help others. But with Pisceans, the sense of ego is usually not strong; in fact, it is quite vulnerable. If a Piscean goes on a search for spiritual wisdom, he or she all too easily can surrender their self (the sense of self) to mind-altering drugs or the dictates of a guru. In normal social interaction they are very exposed to being dominated, through their inner feeling of being obliged to sacrifice themselves for the common good, or for someone close to them.

Hence either the spiritual inclinations, or the socially self-effacing nature of the Piscean, make them very prone to losing their self-hood in mystical self-negating, or through letting others dictate to them. Their over-all gentleness, which causes them to lose out in many encounters and opportunities, is enhanced by the underlying mystical quality of their philosophical attitude. This quality is defined in the lectures in *Human and Cosmic Thoughts*, as "psychism", which Rudolf Steiner defines as the view that all Ideas are linked to spirit beings, in a general sort of way.[56]

In the Lost, may Loss be found,

The thought behind this line is that, if a Piscean loses something, may they perceive that they have indeed undergone a loss. In other words, it is important that they acknowledge this loss. The actual message here appears to be: if the Piscean undergoes a loss, and this does not mean material possessions but aspects of their own soul-life, they should become aware of the loss. The 'lost' referred to here is about loss as such, not a specific object being lost, as the last line makes clear, when it refers to "loss" as an experience, not to something being lost. Any loss that they, as Pisceans, suffer will undermine the integrity of their being. That is, someone has probably deprived them of their social or personal rights; and this is what happens so often to the gentle, self-effacing Piscean.

So this line is saying to the Piscean that, if you lose some of your rights or have your needs disrespected, may you really perceive that this has happened ! This is the first step to preventing repetition of this, and to preventing self-undermining of one's own ego.

In what is gained, may gain be lost !

Here a kind of polar opposite thought occurs, a sign of the turbulent, somewhat chaotic energies associated with the 'descending' zodiacal signs. Here 'lost' is not meant in the sense of a physical object that cannot be found.[57] The thought behind this line is subtle, and appears to have two aspects. Firstly, if a Piscean person gains something, may the gained thing, or acquired quality in their soul, be considered not something that one has gained through their own

---

[56] This is a different definition to that in philosophy, where it is defined in all sorts of ways; generally as an anti-materialism attitude.

[57] This more subtle meaning is caused by the German verb here being a so-called 'reflexive' verb.

merits, nor should it be viewed as for one's own personal gain. In this sense, the line pleads that the gain be viewed as not something to excite vanity, nor selfishness.

The meaning here appears to be: if a Piscean has acquired something, some material gains that come their way, then may such a win be surrendered up to higher purposes. Or, if they have gained spiritually, may they not consider this to be the result of their own efforts, but as a gift of the spirit. So this line is saying to the Piscean that, you have a need to be a selfless, charitable person; and if you do advance spiritually, then consider this to be granted to you from the spiritual world.

In what is grasped may the grasping be sought

Further contemplation of the Piscean ego-sense yields a very relevant meaning to this line. Another translation, which is grammatically quite valid, is often encountered, *'In what is comprehended may the comprehending seek itself'*; but this appears to be inaccurate to what is meant here. Because for the Piscean person, the dilemma is not centred around 'comprehending' but around 'grasping'. People born in this sun-sign are very reluctant to grasp at anything, as they feel impelled to avoid standing up for their own wishes and opportunities.

The Piscean lets other people seize the situation, to the Piscean's detriment. It is important that he or she tries to learn how to take hold of opportunities and also protect their rights. The Piscean needs to learn that when they do on occasion, reach for something (to grasp it), this can be entirely ethical, and indeed they need to seek this ability to grasp, to seize opportunities (or outcomes in life) that are meant for them.

and retain itself in the Retained !   (or, ...in the Maintained / Sustained / Preserved)

This line urges the Piscean to hold on to the capacity to grasp hold of whatever life offers them; and this ability needs to be retained. It needs to become part of those abilities which are retained.

Through Becoming, raised to Being;

As the Piscean person engages in the task of being fully in life, and keeping away from any self-undermining caused by oppression from others, then they move from a developing, growing phase (a 'becoming') into really being in existence.

through Being, interwoven in the Becoming !

Here is another polar opposite idea, the reverse of what the line before was describing. Once the Piscean has fully entered into their life, by exerting their ego, then in fact they do get interwoven into the ongoing evolving of humanity. They enter, to their great advantage, into another 'Becoming'.

The Loss is to be Gain in itself !

The declaration in this last line echoes the messages in the first two lines, and makes the firm statement that, as the Piscean learns the great lessons relevant to this sun-sign, then any selflessness or surrendering to others (or to higher purposes) shall be a true gain for them, and not a self-debasing process. It shall not be a disguised pathway down to the misery of a manipulated and repressed way of life. This line is not <u>entreating</u> '*may* the loss be gain...', rather it is in the 'imperative' mood which commands or declares a fact.

****

Appendix: the word 'erfühlen' in the Leo verse

Here are two further examples of how Rudolf Steiner used this word erfühlen:

> Ich habe das letztemal darauf hingewiesen, aus welchem dumpfen *Erfühlen* diese Ich-Vorstellung eigentlich auftritt. Sie muß gewissermaßen angefeuert werden... (In GA volume 67, p.310, *Das Ewige in der Menschenseele - Unsterblichkeit und Freiheit.*)

> = "I have pointed out last time, from what *faint inner sensing* this mental image of the "I" actually arises. This must be fired up, as it were...."

Or

> ....der alte Tanz. Der alte Tanz war herausgeboren aus einem *Erfühlen* der Naturgesetze, durch eigene Bewegung ein Nachbild dessen, was in der Natur sich bewegte. (In GA 55 p.220 - *Die Erkenntnis des Übersinnlichen in unserer Zeit und deren Bedeutung für das heutige Leben*)

= "...the old dance (type of dancing done in olden times). The old dance was born out of a *faint inner sensing* of the laws of nature, through one's own movements {it became} an imitation of that which was in movement in nature."

At this point, for the sake of completeness, we can consider briefly the fourth set of zodiac images designed by Rudolf Steiner. These are in the large painting from 1911-12, by Anna May, but they were only a small part of this large artwork.

The zodiac images from the Anna May painting

Whereas most of this special painting is quite clear, these zodiac images are only a small part of the huge artwork, and so they could not be photographed with clear detail. So some of these images remain hard to decipher. The images in this painting are not similar to those of Stuttgart nor those in the Calendar of 1912/13. They are partly traditional German images, and partly quite innovative, but not alluding to the great evolutionary journey of humanity.

On the top image, starting for the left is firstly, a graphic for Gemini. This appears to depict two people interacting, perhaps children. Next is a sea-creature, representing Cancer. Interestingly, this animal is not a crab, it is more like lobster, and this is in fact how many older German zodiacs portrayed Cancer, for example on the clock of the Town Hall in the German city of Ulm. The next image is for Leo, and although unclear, it appears to be a lion, looking at the viewer. The graphic for Virgo is unfortunately not clear; but appears to be a woman holding something. The graphic for Libra shows a traditional set of balances. The graphic for Scorpio depicts a scorpion, but facing downwards.

Then on the lower picture, from the left, Sagittarius is depicted as a kind of cross-bow, with perhaps part of an archer holding it. This kind of graphic, which does not include a centaur, is again common in older German zodiac art. Following this is a graphic for Capricorn which is unclear; but it seems to depict the head of fish and underneath the legs of a goat. The next image, for Aquarius, is somewhat unclear, but appears to be a water deity letting water cascade downwards. Next is a clear depiction of two fishes, for Pisces. Then for Aries one can see with difficulty, a ram, which is looking directly at the viewer. Finally, for Taurus there is an unclear drawing of a bull, looking towards its left side.

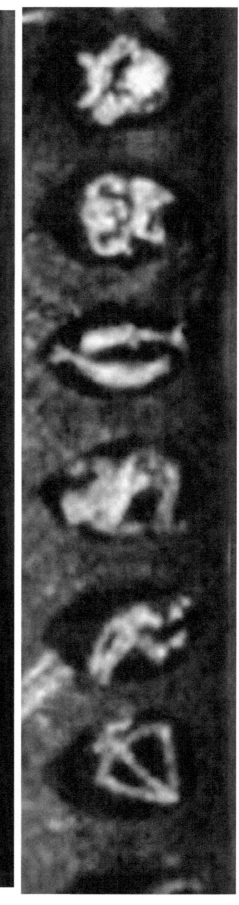

36   The partially blurred zodiac images from the Triptych Grail painting

Designed by Rudolf Steiner, painted by Anna May. The sequence has been separated here into 2 sections for ease of viewing. These images are not clear on the original 1913 photograph. The upper image starts on the left with Gemini through to Scorpio; the lower image starts on the left with Sagittarius and goes through to Taurus.

Appendix One: The Twelve Virtues from H.P. Blavatsky, adopted by Rudolf Steiner

These profound meditative phrases were provided to members of the Theosophical Society in the 19th century. It is assumed that they came from H.P. Blavatsky, that is, provided to her by her guiding Initiate. Rudolf Steiner provided copies of these in his own German translation, to members of the Esoteric School in Germany and elsewhere. He advised that they are to be used from the 21st of the month to the 21st of the next month: this is the cycle of the sun through the zodiac signs or inherent zodiac. (Underneath the English is the German text from Rudolf Steiner.)

Aries:	Devotion *Devotion*	becomes	power of sacrifice *Opferkraft*
Taurus:	Equilibrium *inneres Gleichgewicht*	becomes	progress *Fortschritt*
Cancer:	Unselfishness *Selbstlosigkeit*	becomes	catharsis *Katharis*
Leo:	Compassion *Mitleid*	becomes	Freedom *Freiheit*
Virgo:	Courtesy *Höflichkeit*	becomes	tact of the heart *Herzenstakt*
Libra:	tranquillity *Zufriedenheit*	becomes	Contentment *Gelassenheit*
Scorpio:	Patience *Geduld*	becomes	insight *Einsicht*
Sagittarius:	Control of speech *Gedankenkontrolle*	becomes	feeling for truth *Wahrheitsempfinden*
Capricorn:	Courage *Mut*	becomes	power to release (or redeem) *Erlöserkraft*
Aquarius:	Discretion *Verschwiegenheit*	becomes	power of meditation *Meditationskraft*
Pisces:	Magnanimity *Großmut*	becomes	love *Liebe*

Contemplations On These Meditations
We shall briefly explore the meaning of these words for each sun-sign. Though these meditative words are of value to every person, regardless of their sun-sign, they are especially valuable when a person contemplates the words that apply to their own sun-sign.

Aries: Devotion becomes power of sacrifice

The Aries person seeks to unfold their initiative, to be active. If the assertive Aries person can overcome any tendency to seek power and to have dominance over others in their activity, he or she can attain the capacity to be devoted to a noble cause. Devotion of this sort is a will activity which is selfless; such devotion is a triumph over the lower self. When the urge to dominate is conquered, this allows selflessness in the will (or in the astral urges at least) to arise. It is this achievement that can bestow the capacity to be sacrificial.

Taurus: Equilibrium becomes progress

This meditative verse has a subtle depth to it. Of the three earth signs (Taurus, Virgo and Capricorn) it is the Taurean who has to struggle with inertia in the will, for they are especially phlegmatic. The earth element weighs them down strongly. The other two earth signs don't manifest this problem. The Taurean however, appears to be a relaxed, contented person precisely through this phlegmatic quality. But this phlegmatic quality means that they live in a state of non-initiative, which is an imbalance, considering that each human being possesses a will. Consequently, the Taurean exists naturally in a state where equilibrium is lacking. To achieve an inner balance, or equilibrium, they have to make the effort to have initiative, to be more responsive to life's opportunities. Once they achieve this, then they are making real progress.

Gemini: Perseverance becomes loyalty

For the Gemini person to become someone who perseveres, who achieves a staying power when confronted with burdens and responsibilities, is not easy. He or she has to fight against the inherent sanguine tendencies of this sign, which seek to avoid being involved long-term in any burdensome or challenging task. But once their ego is able to ensure that they stay focussed on a task, and committed to a burdensome obligation, then the capacity for loyalty is reached.

Cancer: Unselfishness becomes catharsis

The sheer intensity of the sentient-soul (that is, the strength of the emotions or feelings) in a Cancerian person makes them emotionally vulnerable. They are traumatized if they are subjected to unloving or unkind behaviour. This dynamic of reacting to real or imagined harshness from others can easily pass over into a selfishness, or a self-centred way of being. But the meditation is saying, if effort is made on the spiritual path to become consciously unselfish, then this inner journey becomes one of catharsis, that is, it leads to purification of the astral body.

Leo: Compassion becomes Freedom

The Leo personality is easily stirred to action, and this means that they are a person of initiative; and this results in them having a prominent role socially. But if compassion for others can be the true motif in any such activity, then he or she can attain to a high achievement: inner freedom. In this state, as Rudolf Steiner describes in his book, *The Philosophy of Freedom*, the impulse towards action is not egotistical, and certainly not autocratic, but arises naturally from an inherent commitment to the common good.

Virgo: Courtesy becomes tact of the heart

The Virgoan is here faced with admonition to rise above pedantic ways of thinking and critical attitudes; these are the more prominent negative features of the Virgo person. They are being urged to achieve courtesy, which one could also call generosity of the spirit in social contexts. That is, when it comes to interacting with, and naturally assessing, other people, the Virgoan is being urged to be empathetic and tolerant. This achievement then leads on to a true 'tact of the heart'.

Libra: Contentment becomes tranquillity

The Libran is subject to a constant awareness of the power of other people's wants and demands, and how this presses on their own sense of self. This produces a resentment and tension around the existential question; can they be true to themselves? For he or she has difficulty in expressing their true opinion, let alone insisting on having their intentions and resolutions respected in contested situations. Once the Libran finds the ego-strength to stand up for their views and resolutions, then an inner contentment arises, and from this, tranquillity can be attained.

Scorpio: Patience becomes insight

The Scorpio person has an inner strength and a steely fire within, which means that the Scorpio person struggles with being patient in irritating social circumstances. When they are particularly annoyed by someone, a cutting remark can quickly put the other person in place. The meditation is advising that if the Scorpio person can find the inner strength to restrain themselves in this situation and to have patience, then they shall develop insight into life and people.

Sagittarius: Control of speech becomes feeling for truth (or, a sense for truth)

The Sagittarian is well known for their lack of diplomacy; they speak up without first considering how their comments will affect the listener. The meditation is advising them to strive to gain sufficient ego-presence to be able to develop a social awareness, which allows them to control how they express their thoughts. If this is achieved, then this faculty can bring about a wonderful metamorphosis in the soul which bestows on the Sagittarian person an enhanced sense for truth.

Capricorn: Courage becomes power to release (or to redeem)

This meditation on Capricorn is more difficult to grasp. A key is found in the German word for courage. As we shall see in the verse for Pisces, there is a similarity between the German words for 'magnanimity' (Großmut) and courage (Mut). This indicates that the need for the Capricorn is not courage in the usual sense, of a soldier at war for example, but the more subtle form, namely of taking the initiative. To have an initiative requires confidence and a subtle courage which allows one to face the social pressures that being active in society requires. It is well known to astrologers that the Capricorn shrinks back from putting themselves in the limelight, but not because of cowardice. There is often a blockage in their soul which prevents them from stepping forward; a kind of social confidence is needed. If this is found, then the power to have a major impact on others (and on one's own soul-life) arises. This appears to be what is meant by the term the "power to release" (or redeem).

Aquarius: Discretion becomes power of meditation

A core feature of Aquarians is their vivacious, enquiring intelligence; they are drawn to new ideas and greatly enjoy discussing ideas - regardless of whether they are committed to the idea or not. So they have a sanguine mentality, and this quality is strengthened by the influence of Uranos, which is now well-known for its way of exacerbating a restless, at times eccentric way of being. So a challenge for the Aquarian person is often this indiscreet way of thinking: that is, they need to be more discerning and to more carefully assess ideas before committing to a viewpoint.

Rudolf Steiner added the German word "Verschwiegenheit" here, a term which implies being discreet by being silent. The Aquarian is being advised here to have more discretion in the way they approach ideas - one could say, to achieve a kind of soul-silence about a new idea for a while, to allow a more insightful contemplation to take place. If this is done, then a deepened, more nuanced way of using their mind can lead to an enhanced ability to meditate.

Pisces: Magnanimity becomes love

Magnanimity is a rare word; it is defined in the Oxford Dictionary as "nobility of soul, being above pettiness, having courage". But when the dictionary gives 'courage' as one aspect of magnanimity, it means that this virtue consists of social courage in terms of generosity and personal confidence; not bravery in a military context. The meditation here is advising that if the gentle Piscean can achieve magnanimity, then the capacity for love can be attained. And love here means 'agape' which is love in the core of the soul, in the will. The Piscean shall have to step out and bravely make an impact on their world to achieve this.

****

Appendix Two: Rudolf Steiner and the Zodiacal Cultural Ages

THE ZODIACAL CULTURAL AGES

We have been contemplating the significance of the zodiac influences for humanity, in a variety of ways. In this Appendix to the book, I present the results of my research into a vexed question for students of anthroposophy concerning the way that Rudolf Steiner presents the flow of history. He describes how humanity's history is determined by the movement of the sun through twelve 'zodiac' sectors, usually called by him 'zodiac signs'. This perspective of Rudolf Steiner means that history is understood to proceed in a series of zodiac-based 'Cultural Ages'. But until now, it has not been possible to determine just what zodiac is Rudolf Steiner using for this timing of history. To answer this question is very important, as the inability to identify the zodiac involved, leaves anthroposophical work open to criticism from society in general.

So, what are the Cultural Ages in anthroposophy? They are presented as cultural influences which commence and cease on precise dates according to a certain zodiac influence. Furthermore, the implication in Rudolf Steiner's teachings is that the spiritual-religious leaders of earlier cultures were aware of these Ages. For example, it is understood that at 2907 BC on the spring equinox morning, the new Age of the Bull occurred, as the sun entered a sector of the heavens associated with Taurus. Prior to this, the sun was in Gemini for 2,160 years. So in anthroposophy it is understood that 2,160 years after the Age of Taurus began, on the spring equinox, the sun entered another zodiacal sector, the one associated with Aries. And again at that time, it is implied in anthroposophy, the main symbol of deity was then changed from that of a sacred Bull to a sacred Lamb (or Ram), because the initiated leaders were aware of this change in the cosmic cycles. This movement of the sun through the zodiac is understood in the modern world as being caused by the so-called 'Precession of the Equinox'.

The Precession of the Equinox

Before we go any further, we need to consider what is the Precession of the Equinox? This term means the precession, or going backwards, of the point on the horizon where the sun is seen to rise on the morning of the spring equinox, each year. One would think that if one observed where the sun rose on the same day each year, choosing the Vernal Equinox Point (which is where the sun rises on the spring equinox), it would always be the same, year in, year out. And to a casual night sky observer that is reasonably true. But actually, when viewed over centuries, the sun's position on the horizon slips slowly backwards.

At this point we need to consider various problems. The anthroposophical view that ancient people noticed, and formally responded to, such zodiacal changes is not supported by historians, because there is very little historical evidence of any change in religious symbols being made as the sun passed from one sign into another. Another objection to the idea of zodiacal Ages is from astronomers, who point out that in the history of early cultures, there is no evidence of the precise, long-term astronomical observations, and the accompanying complex mathematical calculations, that would make prediction of these zodiacal cycles achievable. However, in the 19th century, some German scholars did conclude, even if they could not explain how it was possible, that the ancient Babylonians measured time in zodiacal Ages, because of records concerning their king Nabonassar, (see below).[58]

Furthermore, although the Precession phenomenon is somehow involved in bringing about the Cultural Ages, it **cannot be** the direct **physical** cause of the Cultural Ages, as taught by Rudolf Steiner. Why not? Because the Precession of the Equinox does not proceed in a perfect, totally

---

[58] Alfred Jeremias writes about this in, *Das Alte Testament im Licht des alten Orients,* Leipzig, 1906.

uniform way – the time the sun takes to make this apparent movement from one sign to another actually varies ! **That's right, it varies; it is not always 2,160 years** ! **It is a variable time** ! How is this possible? It is possible because of complex forces, associated with gravity, active in the solar system itself; through these forces the sun can take up to 80 years more, or 80 years less, to go through a sector that we designate as a zodiac sign ! These forces induce an irregular motion (called a nutation) in the Earth's rotational wobble. These forces come for example, from the sun as it crosses the equator at an equinox, and also from the moon as its orbital plane drifts up and down, completing a cycle every 18.6 years.

Because students of anthroposophy have not been able to discover any cosmic process that makes possible these precise epochs, some of his students have decided that Rudolf Steiner had made a mistake, despite his clear assertions that these epochs each last the same length of time. So they now conclude that these epochs are not exactly 2,160 years at all, they can be longer or shorter. The reason for their rejection of Steiner's teachings here, is not only that they could not uncover any underlying cause of such a regular cosmic cycle, but also because scientific astronomical knowledge makes it quite clear that in the cosmos, no such precise, regular celestial cycles can possibly exist. Here we note that this scientific knowledge concerns the physical world, it would not apply to the etheric level of the cosmos.

Nevertheless, I have concluded that Rudolf Steiner is correct, and I shall present the process in the cosmos which I believe underlies these 2,160 Ages. Firstly, with regard to the lack of evidence of temple priest-hoods changing their religious symbols, lack of evidence is not proof that this was not done. It is only proof that, so far, no evidence of this has been found, or perhaps has not been allowed to be acknowledged in academic circles. With regard to a lack of accumulated mathematical and astronomical data needed to calculate the motions of the celestial bodies, this body of work is not needed, as the priesthoods were made aware of these cosmic cycles by their spiritual consciousness, not by observations and scientific methods.

In addition, there are some interesting historical phenomena from old Babylonian sources which may possibly constitute some evidence of people in antiquity acknowledging the zodiacal Ages. As I mentioned in the *Rudolf Steiner Handbook*, this concerns reports about a Babylonian king, Nabonassar (or Nabu-nasir), who ruled from 747-732 BC. A ninth century Byzantine Christian chronicler, George 'Syncellus', reported from fragments of historical documents written by two Hellenistic writers centuries earlier, that in 747 BC king Nabonassar decreed that a new era had begun.[59] Amongst the 800 pages of his document he writes that,

> As from Nabonassar the times of the stars' motions were diligently recorded by the Chaldeans.   (From his CRONOGRAFIAZ, trans. by the author) [60]

And in the same book he also writes,

> King Nabonassar asked for the collecting up of the annals of the kings before him in order that the Chaldean kings before him become purged (from the historical records).[61]

Now the decree from the king for the 'collecting up' of the records of earlier Babylonian kings is understood by some scholars as a prelude to having them destroyed, for personal megalomaniacal reasons. But the Greek verb used here means 'to collect up', and not to destroy. So I have concluded that it is more likely that the king wanted them locked away, in order to inaugurate ceremoniously a new era of time. The significance of these two reports together,

---

[59] Namely Berossus, active about 280 BC and Alexander Polyhistor active in perhaps 90-70 BC.
[60] ... απο δὲ Ναβονασάρου τοῦ Χρόνου τῇ τῶν ἀστέρων κινήσεω Χαλδαῖοι ἠκρίβωσαν ... (ΧΡΟΝΟΓΡΑΦΙΑΖ page 207; 20-21 [p.389 Byzantinae 1832, Bonnae]).
[61] Ναβονάσαρὸ συναγαγὼν τὰ πράξεῖ τῶν πρὸ αὐτοῦ βασιλεων ἠφάνισεν ὅπῶ ἀπ' αὐτοῦ ἡ καθαρίθμησι. γίνεται τῶν Χαλδαιων βασιλέων. (ΧΡΟΝΟΓΡΑΦΙΑΖ page 207;3-5   [p.390 Byzantinae 1832, Bonnae]).

about what Nabonassar decreed in the year 747 BC is suggestive of, if not actual proof of, the official recognition of a new Age (that of Aries) commencing.

This theme is presented further in the *Rudolf Steiner Handbook*, where some other evidence from ancient cultures is briefly presented. Here we shall proceed on the basis that Rudolf Steiner's research is correct, and ask, are these zodiacal influences derived from the passage of the sun through the constellations of the zodiac, or from the zodiac based on the zodiac signs of Ptolemy? **Or, do these influences come from another zodiac?** This question is vital for, as anthroposophists have pointed out, there a time difference of some centuries between the sun entering either a constellation (or a zodiac sector of the ancient Babylonian zodiac) and the beginning of a Cultural Age. The Babylonian zodiac had twelve equal-sized sectors, but these sectors or signs were not the same as those of the 'tropical' zodiac of Ptolemy, nor were they a true sidereal zodiac, that is zodiac sectors copying the constellations, because the constellations are not equal-sized (see below for more about this). One thing is clear; Rudolf Steiner specifically teaches that history proceeds in these precisely dated epochs, each one consisting of exactly 2,160 years, but he did not identify the zodiac involved. Very much in the anthroposophical view of life and the evolving of earthly existence, is based on the length of these epochs.

The Zodiac Ages
Let's see what are the key statements about the Ages in anthroposophy. The sun precesses through 'the zodiac', and so every 2,160 years precisely, it enters a new segment of this zodiac. The dates of this process are given as precise figures. In a simple table form we can see what Rudolf Steiner taught. When the Vernal Point (i.e., the 21st March, the spring equinox day, of the northern hemisphere) occurs in the following years, a new zodiacal Cultural Age began, or will begin:

BC 7227 the Age of Cancer
BC 5067 the Age of Gemini
BC 2907 the Age of Taurus
BC 747 the Age of Aries
1413 AD the Age of Pisces
3573 AD the Age of Aquarius
5733 AD the Age of Capricorn

To find the basis of these Ages, we need to know firstly, that there are several zodiacs. There is the obvious Constellational Zodiac, made up of the star groups through which the sun passes on its pathway (the ecliptic) around the heavens. The second zodiac is the little-known ancient Babylonian zodiac, made up of the twelve constellations divided into equal-sized segments: we can call it the BES zodiac. We will need to remember this Babylonian Equal-sized Segments zodiac (or BES for short), because it is very important with regard to the Cultural Ages, even though it appears to be of little relevance. The third zodiac is the Tropical Zodiac (or Inherent Zodiac), which, as the booklet *The Nature and Origin of the Tropical Zodiac* reveals, is a reflection of the BES zodiac. But this reflection exists as an ethereal energy-field, located around the upper atmosphere of the Earth, not out in galactic space. It is this zodiac that has to be used to create a natal horoscope, see illustration 37.

Now these zodiacal Cultural Ages as presented in anthroposophy do imply that ancient civilizations marked the flow of historical time by the backwards 'precessing' of the sun, seen on the spring equinox each year, through 'the zodiac'. But famously, Rudolf Steiner did not specify which zodiac creates this cosmic clock, and as we have noted, there is no such exactly regular cosmic process. What I have discovered is that **the anthroposophical zodiac Ages are connected to the procession of the equinox, but not as a strictly physical spatial phenomenon**, as understood in modern scientific astronomy. The zodiacal Ages are linked to

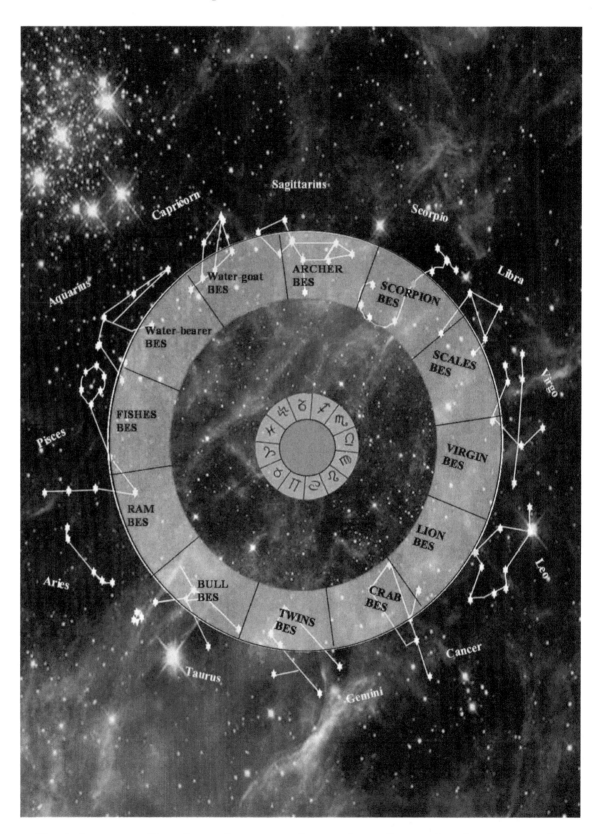

The inherent zodiac shown here in pink, envelops the Earth. The green zodiac is the BES zodiac. The Inherent Zodiac signs receive astral energies from the constellations.

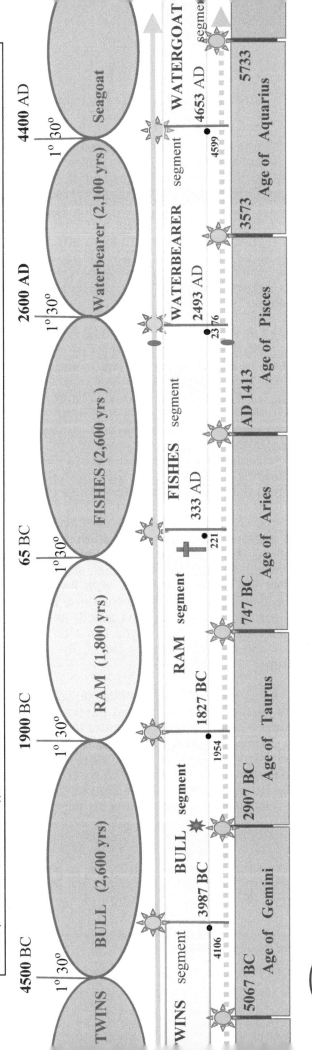

38 The sun through the 3 Zodiacss: on the Vernal Equinox entering the Constellations Zodiac, the Babylonian Equal-sized Segments (BES) Zodiac, & the Cultural Ages Zodiac.   The Inherent Zodiac is not shown.   (The dates of the sun's entry into the constellations are approximate.)

<figure>
TWINS   BULL (2,600 yrs)   RAM (1,800 yrs)   FISHES (2,600 yrs)   Waterbearer (2,100 yrs)   Seagoat
4500 BC   1900 BC   65 BC   2600 AD   4400 AD
1° 30°   1° 30°   1° 30°   1° 30°   1° 30°   1° 30°

WINS   segment   BULL   segment   RAM segment   FISHES   segment   WATERBEARER   segment   WATERGOAT   segment
3987 BC   1827 BC   333 AD   2493 AD   4653 AD
4106   1954   221   2376   4599

5067 BC   2907 BC   747 BC   AD 1413   3573   5733
Age of Gemini   Age of Taurus   Age of Aries   Age of Pisces   Age of Aquarius

BULL segment
3987
</figure>

= The constellations

= The star Aldebaran, in the centre of the BES of Taurus (15°)

= 21st century (shown twice)

The movement of the sun on the Spring Equinox, year after year. Physical sun in yellow, etheric sun in green. They move backwards through the constellations, BES & Cultural Ages zodiac.

The BES or Babylonian Equal-sized Sectors Zodiac. The implied R. Steiner dates of the sun's entry into these are in blue. This BES zodiac has Aldebaran exactly centred in the segment of Taurus, and each segment is of equal size. (Technical note: the SVP of the BES in R. Steiner's view varies slightly from the mathematical model of Fagan & Bradley, their dates are in black.)

Note: 33 AD — the time of Christ
The sunrise vernal equinox point was then at: ca. 29° in the constellation of The Fishes; it had just entered this. And about 4° in the BES of The Ram; so it is about to leave this BES. It is also about one third into the Cultural Age of Aries.

The Cultural Ages Zodiac — its signs/segments are 2,160 yrs. long, & start exactly half-way through the BES sectors (after 1080 yrs), and so they finish exactly 1080 yrs. into the next BES. These sectors derive from these BES, & not created by the variable precession of the equinox; for like the Inherent Zodiac, they are a fixed ethereal template.

5067
Age of Gemini

105

the equinox precession, but in an ethereal way, not in a physical way; this will be explained below.

So, what zodiac sector is the sun entering on these dates? Certainly not a sector marked out by the constellations. The dates of the sun's entry into the constellations varies hugely, since they are of such different sizes. For example, the sun takes 2,600 years to go through the Bull, but only 1,800 years to go through the Ram. They are of various sizes, so the Cultural Ages would also have to be of various lengths of time, which they are not. (Also the constellations don't have a clearly marked boundary, so it is in fact extremely difficult to determine where one ends, and the other begins. The boundary of a constellation is theoretically somewhere in an area of remote, black space.) Nor are the zodiacal Cultural Ages determined by the sun entering the zodiac sectors (or signs) of the tropical or inherent zodiac which is used in horoscopes. For the dates of the sun entering the sectors or signs in either the inherent zodiac or the constellational zodiac are quite different to the dates given by Rudolf Steiner.

Another possible cause of the Cultural Ages is the passage of the sun through the Babylonian BES Zodiac. For the segments or signs of this zodiac are indeed uniform in size, they are each 30 degrees. Since they are of equal size, they do appear to be relevant. But now comes a problem – exactly where do these signs begin and end? We know that the star Aldebaran was positioned by the Babylonians in the middle of their 'sign' of The Bull (which we call Taurus). This has allowed various researchers on this topic – including astrologers Fagan and Bradley, and Indian astrologers on behalf of their Government – to make a reasonable theoretical case for where the signs begin and end, out there in black space, in the BES zodiac.

If we use such data, and then put the dates onto a time-flow chart and see when the sun would enter these 'signs' over the millennia, what happens? We find that they **are close to** the dates of Rudolf Steiner for the Ages, but they don't quite agree with these. But an important clue has now been uncovered ! See illustration 38, and look at the pale blue bar, divided into segments – these are the BES zodiac, the Babylonian Equal-sized Zodiac. Now, just underneath these segments (or signs), you will see some dates written in black. These tell us when the sun would have entered these signs in the most respected dating system for the old BES zodiac, namely the Fagan-Bradley system.[62] But as we have said, these are not quite in harmony with Rudolf Steiner's dates. However, if we use the dates given or implied by Rudolf Steiner for these BES sectors, an astonishing discovery is made. The Cultural Ages zodiac signs all start **exactly half-way through** these BES signs. Look at illustration 38, below the BES sequence, you can see the pink coloured blocks; these are the cultural zodiac Ages – and they start, as you can easily see at a glance, **exactly half-way through** the BES zodiac sectors !

Before we explore this further, we need to just note that this is the reason for another puzzling phenomenon, namely the way that Rudolf Steiner refers to the zodiac signs that govern the Cultural Ages. In most of the approximately 230 occasions when Rudolf Steiner refers to the zodiac and its divisions, in the 360 German books of his Complete Works, **he actually uses the terms 'sign' and 'constellation' interchangeably**. So in one sentence it is the zodiac *sign*, in the next sentence the same thing is called the zodiac *constellation* ! So in a lecture he may refer to the zodiacal Cultural Age of Aries being created when the sun moves through the *sign* of Aries (Tierkreiszeichen, in German), and then, in the very next sentence, says that it is due to the sun moving through the *constellation* of Aries (Sternbilder) !

And this is extraordinary, for these terms normally refer to two separate realities, of course. We understand the sign of Aries to be quite a different thing to the constellation of Aries. So why does he make these terms interchangeable in regard to the cultural epochs? We shall soon find out. Rudolf Steiner taught that the year AD 333 is exactly halfway through the Cultural Age of

---

[62] Cyril Fagan (1896-1970) and Donald Bradley (1925-1974) were keen astrologers with a sidereal bias, whose research into such themes as the precise points of commencement of zodiac sectors is very valuable.

The sun, halfway into the BES of the Bull, conjunct to Aldebaran (orange),
enters the ethereal reflection of this BES and triggers off the **Age of Taurus**.
So now the **Egyptian-Mesopotamian Age** begins.

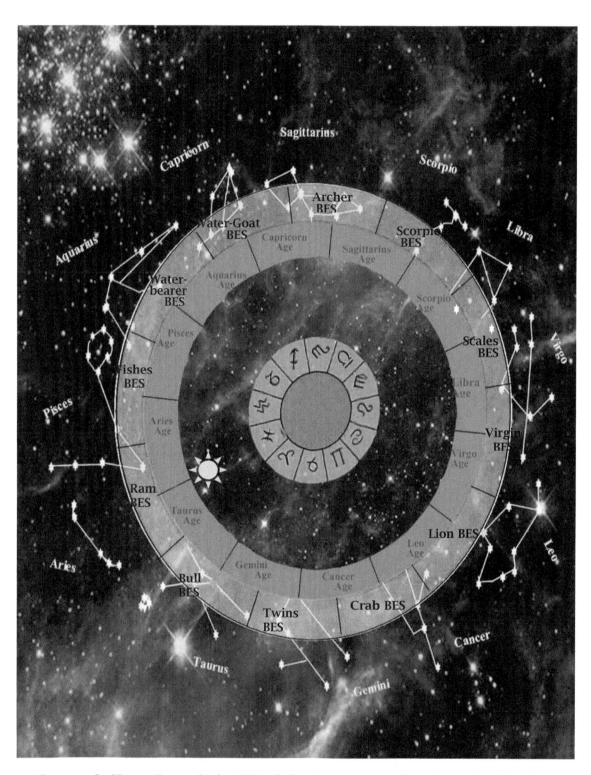

The sun, halfway through the BES of the Ram, enters the ethereal reflection of this BES and triggers off the **Age of Aries**. The **Greco-Latin Age** begins.

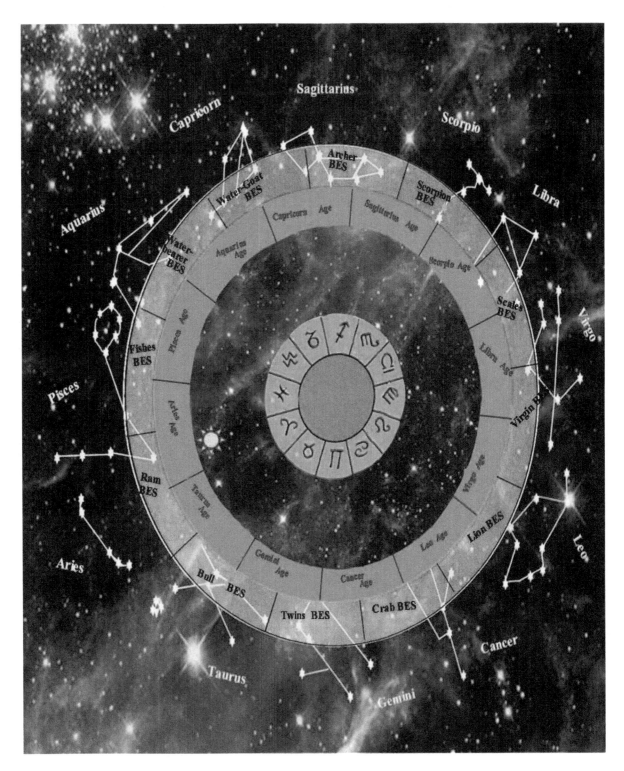

In the time of Christ the sun on 21st March is part way through the Age of Aries and also just into the constellation of the Fishes.

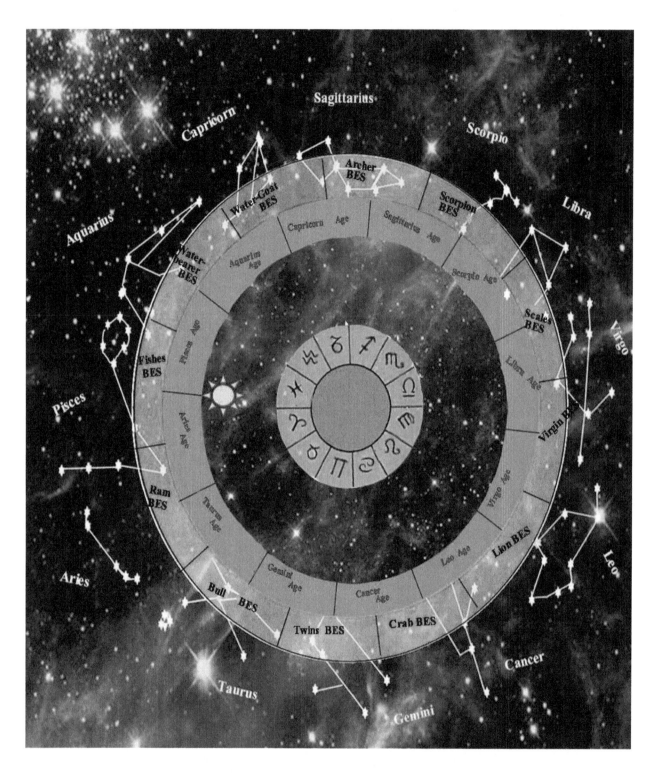

The sun halfway through the BES of the Fishes enters the ethereal reflection of this BES and triggers off the **Age of Pisces**. The Central European/Anglo-American Age begins.

The sun is only one third through the Age of Pisces, but nearly through the Pisces BES sector.

the Ram (Aries), see illustration 38. So, if one notes this statement, and thus slightly adjusts the commonly accepted dates of when the sun enters and leaves the BES of Aries, then we get the dates for all the zodiac signs given here in blue, **and this represents Rudolf Steiner' system !**

This means we need to make only a slight correction to the dates of the best-accepted systems for the old BES zodiac, and then these dates become precisely the dates spoken about (or built upon) by Rudolf Steiner; the dates when the various zodiacal cultural ages begin. It is important to understand that the Fagan-Bradley dates for the BES zodiac are mathematical calculations. They are very capably done, but they are not an exact empirical fact. And what Rudolf Steiner has done, without burdening his audiences to whom the BES zodiac was totally unknown, is to use his knowledge of what are actually the precisely correct figures.

For then the Cultural Ages start exactly half-way through each BES, so Antares is exactly in the centre of the Scorpio BES. And likewise, on the other side of the heavens, forming a potent polarity to Scorpio forces, the star Aldebaran is exactly in the middle of the Taurus BES. As we shall soon see, we have begun to discover the zodiacal basis of the Cultural Ages. Now, it is the case that Rudolf Steiner's dates are definitely given as exact dates; and they are also a prime element of his world-view. There is no room for imprecise data here, for his teachings are based crucially upon the precise accuracy of these dates. So, what is going on?

In the booklet *The Nature and Origin of the Tropical Zodiac* the task was to determine just what is the 'tropical' zodiac, since it is not a physically visible thing; (which has caused astronomers to dismiss it as a mere theoretical idea). In this booklet, it is shown that the 'tropical zodiac' used for horoscopes, (which is better called the 'Inherent Zodiac'), is a reflection of the BES zodiac existing down **in the Earth's ethereal energies**. This is the etheric zodiac that determines our astrological sun-sign, as used in a horoscope. Its twelve sectors are the origin of all the Signs, such as the Sign of Aries, the Sign of Taurus and so on. **But so too there is another ethereal energy field, in which the BES sections are also reflected, but this energy field is far away in space**. And these zodiac sections have the same quality, the same kind of precise geometrical accuracy, as does the Inherent Zodiac. In other words, they are an exact reflection of the BES zodiac, and the sun would 'precess' through them in a precisely predictable, unchanging time-frame (if it were not subject to aberrations in its motions).

There is a gap of exactly 1080 years between the entry of the sun into the BES, and the date when it enters the Cultural Age zodiac sign of the same name. How is this precise, regular timing possible? We have noted that the physical sun goes through the zodiac signs at a slightly irregular speed, yet the zodiacal Ages occur at a very regular, precise time. **Any such precise rhythmical activity in the cosmos is the signature of an ethereal activity:** that is, whether displayed in the interior of an orange or a pomegranate, or similar patterns in many vegetables and fruits, or in the spiral of leaves emerging from a branch, etc., this is derived from an etheric activity.

So here, with these exact zodiacal Cultural Ages, we are not dealing with the physical starry zodiac, but with an invisible **etheric zodiac, a reflection of the BES zodiac sectors**. And we are also dealing with the influence of **the etheric sun. The motion underlying this etheric interaction is not affected by the 'nutational' forces,** these are actually (physical) gravity waves which slow down or speed up the apparent movements of Earth and sun. See illustrations 39,40,41, 42 and 43 which show the movement of the vernal equinox sunrise point over millennia. So there is no variable time gap here, as there is with the physical precession motion. This variable time with respect to the precession of the physical sun against the background of the physical stars means that the gap between the entry of the sun into the physical BES zodiac sign, and the date when it enters the Cultural Age zodiac sign, does vary, indeed up to 80 years. But not so with an etheric process, **for the interaction of the etheric sun with the etheric zodiac could be uniform, because physical gravity waves would not affect it**. Now, let's consider again the way that Rudolf Steiner uses 'sign' and 'constellation' interchangeably.[63] If the phenomenon of the Cultural Ages is caused by the etheric sun passing through the etheric reflection of the BES zodiac, (and this latter is based on the constellations), then actually the divisions or sectors of this 'Cultural Ages etheric zodiac' so to speak, are constellational as to their origin, and yet they exist etherically as separate 'signs' or sectors. So they are both constellational and yet also signs.

Of course at this point one can agree that this invisible energy-field, reflecting the physically visible Babylonian Equal-sized Signs zodiac could exist. But one can ask, why is there this gap between where the etheric reflection is placed, and where the BES zodiac is located? It is this gap that causes the lag between the time the sun enters the BES sign and the Cultural Ages etheric zodiac. In other words, why are the etheric Cultural Ages zodiac signs half-way along from the BES sign ? The answer is found in two lectures by Rudolf Steiner, given in 1917. He explains that there exists a reflection of the zodiac sectors (and this has to mean the BES zodiac) on an ethereal level. He taught that this etheric reflection is by nature spatially displaced from its physical origin. He points out that there exists an ethereal reflection of starry-astral zodiac energies, and that these ethereal energies manifest both a space and a time lag.

Rudolf Steiner and the lag between ethereal zodiac and constellational zodiac
In lectures given in the Christmas of 1917, Rudolf Steiner spoke of how on the evening of Christmas (24th December), the Three Magi, mentioned in the Gospel of St. Matthew, beheld as a spiritual vision: the sun shining in the constellation of Virgo. This is very intriguing, for in late December each year the sun shines in the constellation of Sagittarius, never Virgo. The sun is not shining amongst the stars of the Virgin at Christmas time !

It is always some three months **before** late December that the sun is amongst the stars of Virgo; in fact from mid-September to late October. Yet the three Magi saw the sun shining in the constellation of Virgo at Christmas time. How can this possibly happen? It is possible because they were not looking at the sidereal zodiac, that is, the physical star constellations in the physical skies ! They were looking at **the etheric reflection of the constellational zodiac** in the cosmos. Rudolf Steiner explained that some months after the sun has been in a place in the constellational zodiac, its presence in this zodiac area is to be seen **in the ethers** in that same part of the sky.[64] This large time-lag is brought about by the process of stars' astral energies becoming absorbed and reflected by what he calls the "cosmic ether". This means the etheric energies out in space, beyond our planet's own etheric aura.

Obviously a time lag and a space lag had to occur for the Magi to see a process occurring in Virgo during late December. Whilst the sun was physically in the stars of Sagittarius, in late December, the Magi saw an image of the Messiah shining in an etheric sun, in Virgo. This could only happen if they gazed into the ethereal reflection of the starry zodiac, only there could they perceive the etheric sun (now joined to an image of Jesus) shining in Virgo. So special was this experience, wherein these three Magi or initiated clairvoyant astrologers perceived a sign of the imminent coming of the Messiah and spiritual sun energies, radiant in Virgo, that Rudolf Steiner used this as the new symbol for Virgo, see illustration 44.

He also used this symbol because it presents the essential nature of the Virgoan influence in other ways as well. Now another key feature of the zodiacal Cultural Ages phenomenon, as presented by Rudolf Steiner, shows that it cannot be from the visible BES zodiac, but has an etheric origin. This feature is as follows: it exerts its influence even though the sun **has not yet entered** the associated physical BES zodiac, and it keeps on exerting an influence **after the sun has left that BES**. This may sound complex, but it is not – just see illustration 45.

---

[63] For example, in the German Complete Works Vol. 94 p.76, vol. 99 p. 54, vol. 100 p.105, vol. 110 p. 96, etc.
[64] A lecture of 23 December 1917 in GA 180.

44 Virgo From Rudolf Steiner's 1912 Calendar, with the colours he specified.

45 THE ZODIACAL CULTURAL AGES These start exactly halfway through the BES or Babylonian Equal-sized Segments zodiac

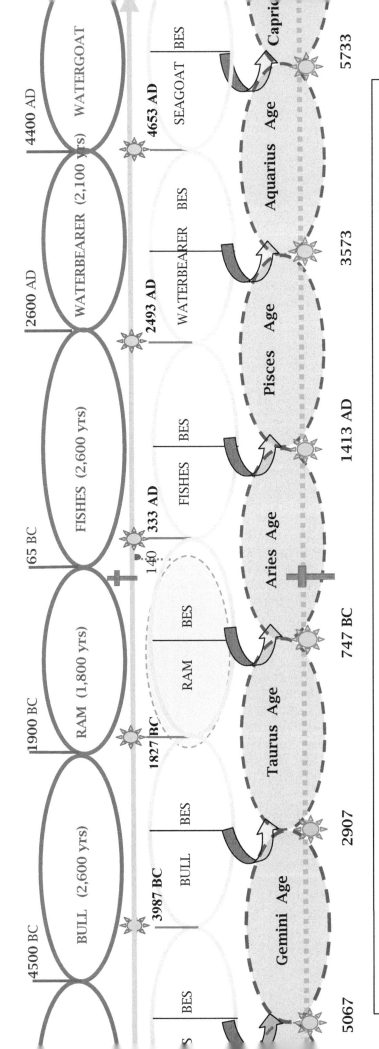

Top section: the **Constellations Zodiac**, showing when the sun enters these, and how long it takes to go through each one (the dates are rounded out) Below this also in blue ovals: the **BES zodiac**, and when the sun enters these.
Superimposed over the Ram BES is one of the **Inherent Zodiac signs**, as a pink oval. This shows how its signs are slightly offset from the BES.
Below this: The **Cultural Ages Zodiac** that create these Ages, and are a reflection of the BES zodiac. These are green ovals to indicate that they
exist in an ethereal energy field. The etheric sun is shown in green, its motion in a green dotted line.
When the etheric sun reaches the half-way point in the BES, it enters the etheric reflection of this BES and a new zodiac Age begins.
The marker for AD 140 refers to the work of Ptolemy, who provided knowledge of the Inherent zodiac at that time.
For clarity, the path of the sun, and the time of Christ and its positions as it enters the signs of the various zodiacs are shown twice.

115

You can see straightaway that the etheric sun has entered, say, the visible BES sector of the Bull in 3978 BC, but not until it is exactly halfway through, in 2907 BC, does the Age of Taurus begin, i.e., the sun then enters the ethereal Sign of Taurus. For the Age of Taurus began in 2907 BC. And yet, the Age of Taurus continued on until 747 BC, even though, already in 1827 BC, the sun had left the Taurean sector and had **physically entered** the BES of the Ram. So the influence starts immediately the ether energies from the sun enter an etheric sign, and it continues until the sun enters a new sign in the etheric field, **despite the sun shining down through the physical BES zodiac.** So the cultural influence occurs from zodiacal astral energies radiating out of the ether, not from physical space.

Consequently, there is no mysterious build-up period involved, requiring complex pentagram gyrations of the planet Venus as postulated in the teachings of R. Powell. The Cultural Age does not start only some centuries after the sun enters a certain constellation or a sign in the BES zodiac, because it has to 'warm-up' by being in that constellation or BES sign for a while.

The Cultural Age starts immediately the sun enters the etheric zodiac, and each sector in this zodiac is positioned half-way along the corresponding BES zodiac signs. So the influence of the etheric Cultural Ages zodiac, like that of the etheric Inherent Zodiac, exerts its efficacy into the human soul, regardless of the physical (sidereal) zodiac. When it is a matter of human consciousness, the etheric zodiac influence always over-rides the sidereal influence. And it exerts this influence as soon as the etheric sun enters the etheric zodiac sign, formed as a reflection of the BES zodiac sign. This process is similar to what happens in the horoscope, based on the tropical zodiac. The positions of the planets and the sun in the etheric Inherent Zodiac exert their efficacy in the new-born infant's astral body, as soon as it is born, conditioning its soul qualities. **Likewise the position of the sun (the etheric sun, one could say) in the etheric Cultural Ages zodiac exerts its efficacy in the minds or astral bodies of humanity, as soon as it enters this etheric sign, subtly conditioning the mental-cultural atmosphere of the Age.**

It is important to realize at this point that there is a very significant reason for the Vernal Point (the sunrise on the vernal or spring equinox day) being chosen as the decisive day. This is because it is on this day that the hemisphere (not the entire dual-hemispherical Earth) then conceives, as it were, the etheric and astral energies streaming in from the cosmos. As my book, *Living A spiritual Year*[65] explains;

> "If another day of the year had been chosen for these yearly observations, say the 22nd of June, then the zodiac sign would have been quite different; it would have been the midsummer time and thus a different zodiac sign would have been behind the sun. The 21st of March is, in the northern hemisphere, the spring equinox day, that time in the spring out-breathing when the hemisphere is especially receptive to the solar forces, which then bring the renewal of the life processes. In earlier times, humanity was aware that this situation has a significance regarding the influence of the zodiac forces. When the hemisphere is so receptive to the cosmos, then the zodiac influences 'behind' the sun also stream into the hemisphere, and become part of the creative forces renewing life on earth.

> It is therefore not surprising that Rudolf Steiner found that in earlier times people felt that the fresh young power of the springtime united with the zodiac force 'behind' the sun. He told one audience that in earlier times people felt that, the zodiac force is the bestower of the sun with its new vigour, it is the bestower of the new creative divine power. In effect, the zodiac force behind the sun at the time when the hemisphere has its spring equinox is uniquely powerful, and it influences civilization in that hemisphere for as long as the sun, at the equinox, is in front of it.

---

[65] This book has been re-published in a revised, expanded version in 2016.

This process has a cycle of 2,160 years, the length of time that the etheric sun takes to move from one part of the (etheric) zodiac to another. Although the northern hemisphere has moved from the Aries age into the Piscean age, and will next move into the age of Aquarius, in the southern hemisphere we are in the age of Virgo and will next move into the age of Leo. The qualities of the Piscean and Virgoan ages are not our present theme, but I have mentioned this subject as an example of how the reality of the cycle of the year will elude us so long as we think in an abstract way about the spiritual reality of the cosmos."

Looking at illustration 45 again, we can see that the sun enters the BES of the Fishes in 333 AD. As we noted earlier, Rudolf Steiner taught that AD 333 is exactly halfway through the Cultural Age of the Ram (Aries). So therefore AD 333 is exactly 1080 years after the Age of the Ram started, and therefore the implication from Rudolf Steiner here is that the BES of the Ram started in 1827 BC, as shown in the diagram, (and not 1954 BC, as Fagan-Bradley concluded).[66]

So Rudolf Steiner, when introducing the concept of zodiacal cultural Ages, has just used knowledge of these points which he has gained from his initiation consciousness. His audience would have been unnecessarily confused if he had attempted to explain the various zodiacs and how they relate to each other. He has mentioned the dates for the cultural Ages without referring to the complex issues involved. There are severe mathematical-astronomical problems surrounding the challenge for astronomers working on this subject. They have to try to work out just at what tiny point in the black night skies, these BES boundary positions are located, from data preserved in ancient Sumerian and Babylonian records, and then relate this to modern astronomical knowledge.

The assumption that the Cultural Ages are caused by the Precession of the Equinox has always implied that the ancients had achieved the sophisticated scientific calculations necessary to work this out. But, as we noted earlier, such mathematical knowledge was not necessary, if the perspective is accepted that the leaders of the ancient Mysteries possessed an intuitive or indeed psychic perception.

The beginning of the Age of Aquarius

We can now be confident that the start of a Cultural Age, as put forward by Rudolf Steiner, is brought about by the entry of the etheric sun into the ethereal Cultural Ages zodiac which is a reflection of the BES zodiac. With regard to the Age of Aquarius, this will occur in AD 3573. The sun shall then enter the Cultural Ages etheric zodiac sign of Aquarius. The popular idea that this Age is to start early in the 21st century is incompatible with the research of Rudolf Steiner. Some people may have decided that this is timed by the sun's entry into the constellation of Aquarius. But that event won't happen until about AD 2600.

To see how impractical is the idea of the Aquarian Age starting soon (e.g., 2012, or 2300, etc) see illustration 46. There we can see exactly that the two constellations of The Fishes and the Water-bearer actually **overlap each other.** So the sun will move into Aquarius, whilst it is actually still amongst the stars of Pisces, **and this overlapping situation will last for more than a century** ! And the same situation prevails in regard to the border between other constellations, in fact even more so! A zodiac age can never occur through the passage of the sun through the Constellational Zodiac, for there is almost always some over-lap, and occasionally these last for hundreds of years.

---

[66] Nor, according to the way Rudolf Steiner used it, did it start in 1946 BC, one of various dates which can result from altering the mathematical data used to determine the BES positions. (Technical note: there are various choices of Ayanamsa & SVP available, each giving slightly different dates; none of these are mathematically absolute.)

The value of the Babylonian zodiac

Having seen the nature of the Inherent Zodiac and the Cultural Ages zodiac as reflections on an ethereal energy level of the Babylonian Equal-sized Sectors zodiac, we can take a moment to feel our gratitude and respect for the leaders of the Babylonian Mysteries who perceived so accurately the existence of the BES zodiac. And also to feel how unwise it is of the modern scientific astronomer to suggest that there are 13 constellations and that the Babylonians got it wrong in regard to the basic fact of how many zodiac constellations there are. (The question Ophiuchus as a 13th sign is discussed in the book, *The Nature and Origin of the Tropical Zodiac.*)

Now to have clarity about these zodiacs, look at illustration 45 again, where we see the BES with their dates as implied by Rudolf Steiner. The structure of this BES zodiac, from ancient Mesopotamia, is based on having the star Antares in the centre of Scorpio. And below the BES zodiac, in green ovals with a red dotted outline, are the ethereal reflections of the BES, creating the Cultural Ages. The green colour is to indicate that these exist in a realm of ethereal life-energies; it is the same kind of energy that underlies the green plant-world of the Earth.

Let's consider the Inherent Zodiac again, and clarify its relation to the other zodiacs and the time-chart. We noted earlier that the phenomenon of an energy reflection of the sidereal BES zodiac underlies the Cultural Ages zodiac, and that this same general kind of etheric reflection is also the basis of the Inherent Zodiac. But the Cultural Ages etheric zodiac is far removed in space, whilst the etheric Inherent Zodiac is located around our planet.

So, the Cultural Ages zodiac is a reflection of the BES, it exists as an ethereal energy-field, in the cosmos. The passage of the etheric sun through the signs of this zodiac create the influences that lead to the Cultural Ages, each lasting for exactly 2,160 years.

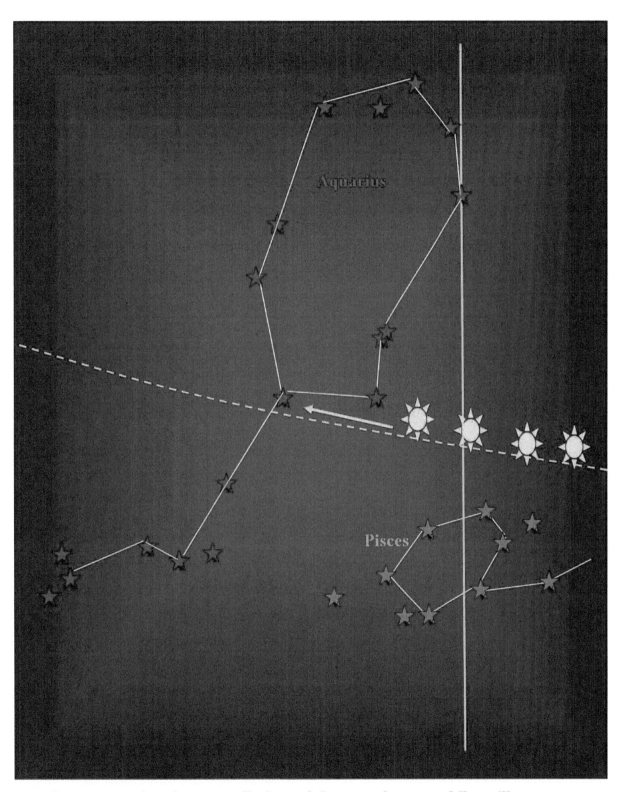

The sun entering the constellation of the Waterbearer, whilst still amongst the Fishes. The green line shows the sun that will still be in Pisces for more than a century after entering the constellation of Aquarius.

Appendix Three: Rudolf Steiner's use of the Inherent-tropical Zodiac

The sidereal zodiac is simply a term for the twelve visible star constellations through which the sun appears to move throughout the year. The term 'tropical zodiac' refers to the twelve signs of the zodiac which are used in astrology; they form the basis of the horoscope. Criticism of the tropical zodiac system arises from time to time by astronomers or a few astrologers who do not feel the validity of this age-old system and who use instead the sidereal zodiac. This rejection is due to the fact that the zodiac signs are based on twelve equal-sized sectors in space, which are not connected to the constellations that they are named after. That is, these sectors or signs are not in the same place in space as the constellations. So to today's scientific mindset, the 'tropical' zodiac is only some theoretical idea, which has no basis in reality.

If you attempt to learn the definition of these two systems in authoritative academic books and encyclopaedias, you gain the impression that the learned writer is unaware that he or she is actually unclear about what they are attempting to define. So there is no clear description of the tropical zodiac available in these books. For somehow, this zodiac eludes all understanding by otherwise capable and informed researchers. The reason for this is that the word 'tropical' is wrongly applied to it. The 'tropical' zodiac has only a minor link with the tropics of Cancer or Capricorn. But learned articles attempt to explain the tropical zodiac by referring to these two tropics, and hence to the seasonal cycle; this leads to deep confusion.

There is only one publication which explains the tropical zodiac: my booklet, *The Nature and Origin of the Tropical Zodiac*. In this booklet, the breakthrough was achieved by a careful study of ancient Greek texts, and merging this with an awareness of the existence of the ether, as distinct from the astral, and physical realms. This brings a solution to the difficult question of just how can the tropical zodiac be valid, if it does not exist – physically, that is. How can it be valid if it is only a theoretical construct?

The above booklet confirms that the tropical zodiac used in a horoscope is not a theoretical idea, but is fully valid, because it exists as **an etheric zodiac**, and was known in the initiatory wisdom of the Hellenistic Mysteries. The tropical zodiac is much more accurately referred to as the **Inherent Zodiac**, because it exists as an etheric reflection of the sidereal zodiac, inherent in the Earth's upper atmosphere; not out in galactic space. It is an etheric zodiac existing in the ether aura of the Earth. Each sign in the Inherent Zodiac receives and activates astral energies from the corresponding zodiac constellation (or sidereal zodiac).

For anthroposophists, the question arises, how did Rudolf Steiner relate to the so-called tropical zodiac signs, the zodiac used in horoscopes? We need to know about this, when contemplating his remarkable new images. Did he use them, and thereby validate them, or did he only validate the sidereal zodiac, the zodiac based on the constellations? In response to incorrect ideas spreading about these subjects, from various New Age siderealist astrologers, we need to consider this question.

People around the globe who have taken up Rudolf Steiner's wisdom are often aware of only two statements from him about astrology: one is to the effect that astrology is a dilettante, fossilized body of knowledge. The second is that a person could interfere with the karma of a client by using the horoscope. And therefore for 90 years the conclusion has often been, that it is "un-anthroposophical" to be involved in it. But those with this view are not so aware of other comments from Rudolf Steiner which show just how valuable horoscope analysis could be, if carried out with spiritual insight. And in these comments he means the Inherent Zodiac, not the sidereal. For example, in September 1905 he wrote,

The real astrology is however a thoroughly intuitive science and demands from those who want to practise it, the development of a higher, spiritual power of cognition. A capacity which in modern times can only be available to the smallest number of people.[67]

In a lecture in 1915, he reiterated his attitude that astrological analysis when carried out by a person who strives after wisdom is a very valid and valuable thing,

> ...I have often said, astrology is either the purest amateurism or it can only be achieved as the end result of a really deep immersion in spiritual-scientific studies and cognizance.[68]

His over-all perspective is found in an archive document, not yet published. It is the answer he gave to a question put to him after a lecture in 1905. He told his questioner whose question is unrecorded,

> What one finds in the manuals on astrology has nothing to do with what the expert knows about these things. I would have to develop the basic concepts {for you to understand what I mean}. The caricature of astrology {of the early 20th century} is something about which one can say nothing. When one comes to know esoteric astrology and becomes knowledgeable about the interconnectedness of people and the cosmos, then one arrives at the possibility to answer the question. As you know, the plants can only grow under the influence of the sunlight. If the sun were to be extinguished, the plants could not grow. The research of the spiritual interconnectedness is approximately what one has to understand 'astrology' to be. [69]

(translated from the unpublished manuscript by the author)

Two important points stand out here. Firstly this was spoken back in 1905, long before astrological analysis went through a thorough renewal, becoming deepened and matured. The profoundly insightful body of knowledge that is now available is vastly superior to the rather elementary formulaic data used over a century ago. Secondly, what Rudolf Steiner meant by researching the spiritual interconnectedness of humanity and the cosmos has only been achieved to a small extent, apart from what he himself achieved. He was to go on from 1905 until 1924, developing a vast body of knowledge about the cosmos and humanity, which is without equal in the modern world.

I am one of the pioneers merging the valuable knowledge developed by astrologers for psychological profiling in the last 40 years, with the extensive body of profound knowledge created by Rudolf Steiner concerning the significance of the planets and the zodiac for human psychology. A counsellor, who wisely uses the tropical horoscope with a client, can do so without interfering in the karma of the client; it is a question of inner tact and maturity. An extensive knowledge of Rudolf Steiner's work enables a very substantial deepening and clarifying of what a horoscope can reveal about the personality.[70] To find out how one can interpret the horoscope, in the light of anthroposophy, see my book, *Horoscope Handbook – a Rudolf Steiner Approach*. It is the result of 25 years consultancy in this area of work. In addition to the above quotes, there are many other examples of Rudolf Steiner directly affirming the tropical (inherent) zodiac. We have already explored a very major work by Rudolf Steiner on the tropical zodiac; that is, the Twelve Moods. Let's consider some more of these,

---

[67] In vol. 34 page 396.
[68] In vol. 162 page 20.
[69] From a Question & Answer session, for lecture March 1905 (archive document).
[70] My Doctoral thesis identifies and explains the primary elements of Rudolf Steiner's worldview. It is available from the university that requested permission to publish it, "*Dramatic Anthroposophy*" from Otago University, website: http://www.otago.ac.nz/german/OtagoGermanStudies/home.html It is vol. 19 on their list.

leaving until last another very major work of Rudolf Steiner's, using the tropical (inherent) zodiac.

Further examples of Rudolf Steiner using the 'tropical zodiac'

ONE
In a lecture in 1916, Rudolf Steiner suggested that someone could draw up the horoscope for central Europe, during the time of the crises in the 1840-1850's, and also draw up the horoscope of H. P. Blavatsky (born 1831). Then by comparing these two charts, one would see what kind of soul qualities she had, and how these qualities were inwardly linked to the dynamics active in Europe of her times.[71] This means using the normal tropical charts, as he did not stipulate sidereal charts - which would have been a startling and memorable thing to require.

TWO
Another example of Steiner's confirmation of the Inherent Zodiac occurred when, to help him assess two people who were born as albinos, he requested that their horoscopes be drawn up. These horoscopes were based on the normal tropical zodiac (the Inherent Zodiac). These two charts are reproduced here, both as inherent zodiac and as sidereal zodiac charts. Steiner commented briefly on these charts. Looking at one of the charts he pointed out that, "the Moon was in Libra". Then looking at the other chart he commented, "and here the Moon is in Libra too"; see illustrations 47 and 48.

With the younger albino person's chart, the Moon was in the tropical Sign of Libra (the Inherent Zodiac). Hence Rudolf Steiner **was directly confirming that the appropriate zodiac to use is the Inherent Zodiac.** Because if a sidereal chart had been drawn up, the moon would have been in the constellation of Virgo, at this time. **And since it was correct to have the moon in the tropical sign of Libra, this means that all the other planets were also correctly situated in the tropical signs.** This fact cannot be disputed; his statements here **completely confirm that the tropical zodiac is the correct zodiac to use for a horoscope.**

However as it happens, the Moon in the older person's chart was in fact ¼ of one degree into the sign of Virgo, so it was on the cusp between Libra and Virgo. But the hand-drawn chart had the moon drawn sitting right over this cusp, and it was unclear to the observer that it was meant to show the Moon positioned just inside Virgo: it looked as if the moon was still in the sign of Libra. So in both cases Rudolf Steiner was confirming the Inherent Zodiac, despite the unclear layout of the second chart; he was meant to understand, when looking at the chart, that the Moon was in the Sign of Virgo. And of course this means that the positions of all the other planets in the Inherent (tropical) charts are a true expression of these persons' personality. And this confirms that the positions of the planets in a sidereal chart would be incorrect to the two personalities.

Unfortunately, a siderealist astrologer, Robert Powell, writes that since the Moon in the second chart was actually in the stars of Libra, the sidereal zodiac is therefore actually the correct zodiac to use, because Rudolf Steiner said the Moon was in Libra. (!) But already Steiner has confirmed the tropical zodiac was correct; and this other statement was simply due to a wrong impression given to him, from the unclear horoscope.[72] This analysis of these charts, and the other examples given here, show that to Rudolf Steiner the Inherent Zodiac is the appropriate zodiac to use, not the sidereal, as any professional astrologer would expect.

---

[71] Rudolf Steiner, Complete Works (GA) vol. 171, p. 234.

[72] Although one notes that the difference between the two charts (tropical or sidereal) for the older person is not as great as with the younger, because with the older person the sun and the moon are in both the sign and the constellation of Virgo.

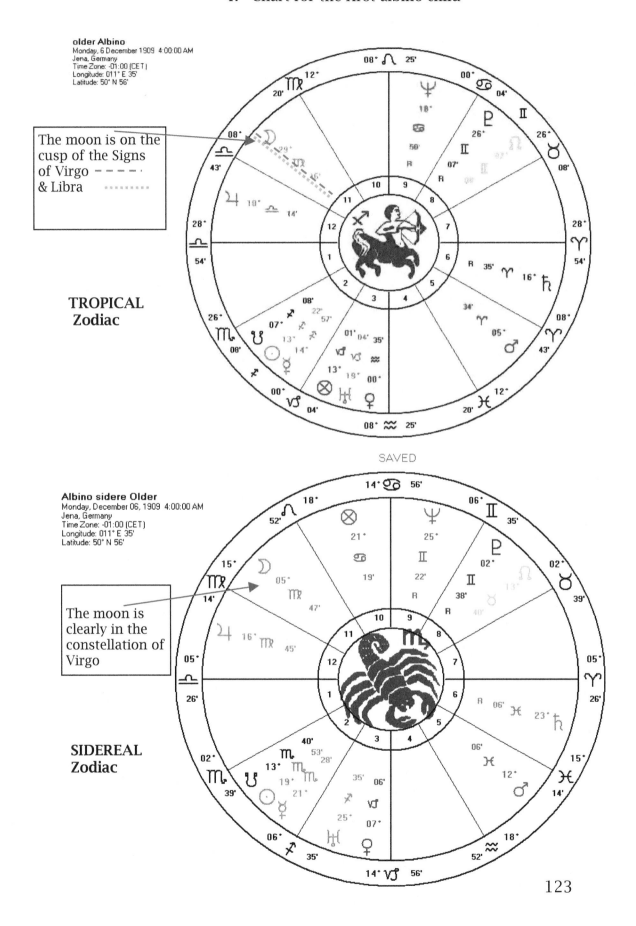

older Albino
Monday, 6 December 1909 4:00:00 AM
Jena, Germany
Time Zone: -01:00 (CET)
Longitude: 011° E 35'
Latitude: 50° N 56'

The moon is on the cusp of the Signs of Virgo – – – – & Libra ....

TROPICAL Zodiac

SAVED

Albino sidere Older
Monday, December 06, 1909 4:00:00 AM
Jena, Germany
Time Zone: -01:00 (CET)
Longitude: 011° E 35'
Latitude: 50° N 56'

The moon is clearly in the constellation of Virgo

SIDEREAL Zodiac

TROPICAL Zodiac

Younger Albino
Wednesday, 18 May 1921 3:00:00 AM
Jena, Germany
Time Zone: -01:00 (CET)
Longitude: 011° E 35'
Latitude: 50° N 56'

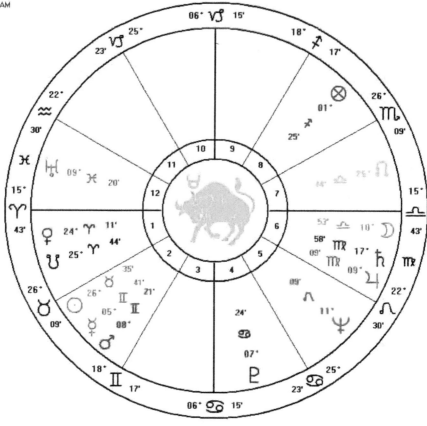

SAVED

SIDEREAL Zodiac

Younger Albino sider
Wednesday, May 18, 1921 3:00:00 AM
Jena, Germany
Time Zone: -01:00 (CET)
Longitude: 011° E 35'
Latitude: 50° N 56'

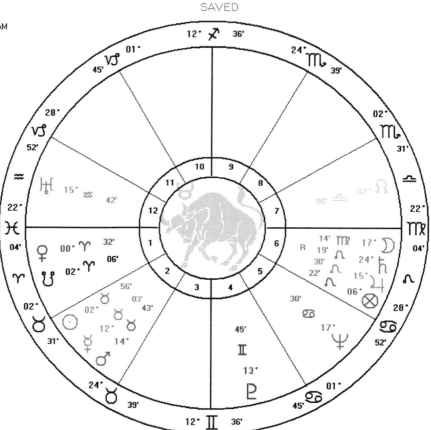

THREE

Moreover, on at least one occasion Steiner sent one of his students, Liselotte Prinz of Stuttgart, to consult an astrologer to get advice about their life-questions.[73] This astrologer, along with all European astrologers throughout history, would have used the Inherent Zodiac. This is another example of Rudolf Steiner validating the tropical zodiac.

FOUR

A particularly strong example of Steiner confirming the tropical zodiac for the horoscope concerns one of his chosen assistants, Franz Seiler (1868 -1959), who lived in the same building in Berlin as Rudolf Steiner, and was often in the small party that went for walks with him. Seiler took official stenographic notes of some 800 lectures, and helped in administrative capacity in many ways, for about a decade. He moved to Dornach when Rudolf Steiner moved there. Seiler was a proficient and learned astrologer, using the Inherent Zodiac.

As his obituary notices reported in the German Anthroposophical Society Journal and the Swiss anthroposophical Journal, Seiler was intensely involved in astrological research with Rudolf Steiner, who encouraged and helped him in his medical astrological research with individual tropical horoscopes.[74] The previous head of the Anthroposophical Society, Manfred Schmidt-Brabant, previously from Berlin, estimated that there were several hundred such horoscopes which Rudolf Steiner helped Herr Seiler research.[75]

FIVE

Rudolf Steiner was also in the audience during a Theosophical Conference in 1907, when Alan Leo, the prominent Theosophical astrologer, gave a lecture on astrology. Steiner's written report praises the pioneering work done by Leo – who used the Inherent Zodiac, of course. He wrote that Alan Leo "spoke in an illuminating way about the question of Astrology and personal fate".[76]

SIX

Very importantly, as we have already seen, Rudolf Steiner gave two sets of meditative verses to his students to assist them to enter more consciously into **the experience of the Inherent Zodiac**. These are the "Twelve Virtues" and of course, he also gave the "Twelve Moods". He specifically made instructions to the effect that **both of these meditative verses are to be meditated upon whilst the sun passes through the relevant Sign of the tropical Zodiac;** the meditation is to begin on the 21st of each month, and this is a simple formula to coordinate them to the tropical zodiac or zodiac signs, as these mostly end or start on 21st/22nd of the month.[77]

The "Twelve Virtues" are formally noted as to be used on the dates of the tropical zodiac in the volume in the Complete Works where they appear. As we have noted earlier, the other meditations, the "Twelve Moods" are also specifically to be used on the dates of the tropical zodiac. This fact is disclosed in a written report in the *Journal of the German Anthroposophical Society* by a student of Rudolf Steiner, Ernst Lehrs, who asked him about this. And the official Anthroposophical Society *Star Calendar* journal, published in Dornach at the Goetheanum, also reports in an article on these verses that when asked by others, Rudolf Steiner declared them to be used on the dates of the tropical zodiac.[78]

---

[73] Reported in *Rudolf Steiner und die Astrologie*, by H.H. Schöffler, R. Geering Vlg, 1996, p. 40.

[74] Mitteilungen aus der Anthroposophischen Arbeit in Deutschland, Easter 1960, Nr. 51, p. 39 and Blätter für Anthroposophie 1959, Dezember, Nr. 12, p. 447.

[75] Schmidt-Brabant's comment published in *Mitteilungen aus der anthroposophischen Arbeit in Deutschland*, 1991, p. 61.

[76] GA 35, Rudolf Steiner's report on the Theosophical Soc. Congress in Munich, of 1907, p. 606.

[77] These dates do **not** relate the dates of when the sun enters during the year the BES zodiac signs or sectors; that varies from around the 14th to 18th of a month.

[78] Sternkalender, Oster, 1967/68, *Die Zwölf Stimmungen von Rudolf Steiner* Suso Vetter, ps. 83-84.

Naturally it is incorrect to think that these verses are only relevant to the northern hemisphere, because the Inherent Zodiac signs are applicable to the entire Earth. To conclude that no-one born in the southern hemisphere could ever have a proper Inherent Zodiac horoscope drawn up, because this zodiac is simply a seasonal thing,[79] and is only valid for the northern hemisphere, is simply a conclusion that a professional consultant who uses the tropical horoscope could never make. As the booklet about *The Origin and Nature of the Tropical Zodiac* observes, it is a fact that the horoscope is fully valid for your personality, regardless of which hemisphere you were born in.

But in so far as the direct influence of the stars has an impact on the plant life and on animals, Rudolf Steiner's bio-dynamic agriculture methods are based on the sidereal zodiac. And he wanted to help his students also to gain an ability to sense the subtle energies of the starry heavens, and the effect of the planets moving through them. So he gave advice on entering **into a feeling for the visible (sidereal) zodiac.**[80] The use of a sidereal horoscope is entirely contrary to Steiner's teachings. So the conclusion by R. Powell that those who oppose sidereally based horoscopes "form the hosts of Klingsohr", is without foundation.[81] Klingsohr is the name of an evil enemy in the Holy Grail sagas, and as such, is to be regarded as a particularly vile person. From the above evidence, this statement would in effect, unwittingly, include Rudolf Steiner as among these hosts, as he used and recommended the tropical astrology for horoscopes.

But as we have noted in these six examples, Rudolf Steiner affirms that all of our soul qualities are made manifest by the Inherent Zodiac – and that is what a horoscope, based properly on the tropical or inherent zodiac, reveals. When we consider the seventh example of Rudolf Steiner's usage of the inherent or tropical zodiac, the confusion behind the sidereal attitude will become even clearer. In general terms, the sidereal zodiac can be about 15% aligned to the tropical zodiac, as the signs and the constellations can overlap a little. So a small amount of accuracy can accidentally arise. But the sidereal can never provide a detailed accurate profoundly insightful guide to the personality.

It is important for the facts about the tropical (inherent) zodiac to be known, because as the book *The Nature & Origin of the Zodiac* reveals, the tropical zodiac was known to the initiates, it was a central topic of the ancient Mystery wisdom. By the professional use of this zodiac in therapeutic consultations, invaluable help could be offered to people seeking help or self-knowledge.

As we have seen above, Rudolf Steiner endorsed, made use of, and directly confirmed, the use of the tropical natal horoscope. But he was discreet with his affirmation of horoscope interpretation, as he was opposed to the superstitious and unthinking way that early 20th century astrology was often practised. But he did confirm completely the validity of the Inherent Zodiac for the horoscope.

SEVEN
Perhaps the most potent example of Rudolf Steiner using and working spiritually with the tropical zodiac, that is the inherent zodiac, concerns the great and pivotal moment in his life when he decided to build the Goetheanum. This process started with a powerful spiritual event, in which he stood on the bare field from which the building was to arise. He gave an electrifying speech to the small crowd gathered around him in the darkness, and he also had brought some

---

[79] As is stated by R. Powell.
[80] For example, two students, Margot Rößler and Imme von Eckardstein reported on his help in this regard, in Mitteilungen aus der Anthroposophischen Arbeit in Deutschland 13. Jhrg Heft 1 Ostern 1959. p. 26.
[81] "..It is the forces of Klingsohr, referred to by Rudolf Steiner, which are at work. These 'Klingsohrian forces' seek to perpetuate a decadent astrology and are able to work all the more effectively as long as ignorance and illusion prevail, as is the case in modern astrology with its adherence to the tropical zodiac." In the journal *Anthroposophy Today*, p. 29, "Towards a new wisdom of the stars" R. Powell. 1991.

parchment on which he had drawn an illustration and written some profound cultic words about the inter-weaving of the hierarchies in this process. He had specially chosen the day and the time of day for this event, it was not randomly chosen, as the words on the parchment reveal. The relevant part of his address is this:

"Let us rightly understand what we are doing – on this stone, as our corner-stone, there is also stated as the wording of our vow –

the human being who wills to –
seek itself in Spirit
feel itself in the Soul of the Cosmos
intuit itself in the I of the Cosmos.

This stone we now place down in the densified realm of the elements
as a symbol of the Power towards which we are seeking to strive, through
....three, five, seven, twelve [82]

Placed by the St. John's Building[83] Association, Dornach on the 20th day of September 1880, after the Mystery of Golgotha; i.e., 1913 AD, **as Mercury was present in Libra as the evening star.**"

Now exactly where was Mercury on that day ? It was in Steiner's words, "in Libra". But was it in the **constellation** of Libra or the **Sign** of Libra ? **It was in the tropical Sign of Libra** ! (Sidereally, it was amongst the stars of Virgo at this time.) So the cosmic influences and timing which Rudolf Steiner wanted to align this event with, was the planet Mercury being in the Sign of Libra. Obviously to Rudolf Steiner the tropical zodiac was not irrelevant, as some sidereal sources state, rather it was a central part of human life and that includes the cosmic timing of great spiritual events. You can see a copy of this drawing on the next page.

This seventh example of Rudolf Steiner's use of the tropical zodiac is a powerful one. It establishes beyond argument that in anthroposophy, the inherent zodiac is a central factor in humanity's link to the zodiacal reality.

The parchment drawing placed inside the concrete housing of the Foundation Stone for the First Goetheanum

This diagram shows the interweaving of divine-spiritual beings in the creating and sustaining of humanity. The names of the nine ranks of hierarchical beings are given by the first one or two letters of their name. But it is the last words here which are so significant: "da Merkur {shown as a symbol} als Abendstern in der Waage stand".

This means: "when Mercury was there as the evening star in Libra". This was the **Sign** of Libra, not the constellation. So the timing of the laying of the Foundation Stone of the Goetheanum was based on the tropical-inherent zodiac.

---

[82] Rudolf Steiner spoke these numbers, and later struck the copper dodecahedron that number of times.
[83] Literally, the Johannes Building Association, but St. John is perhaps the more correct English rendering.

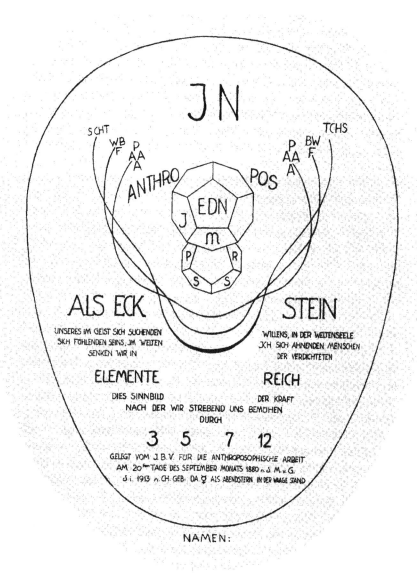

Horoscope interpretation

Sadly, many students of Rudolf Steiner are unfamiliar with the extremely valuable psychological profiling work from the horoscope that has been achieved over the past 60 years; they are focused more on the significance of the Constellations Zodiac. (And sadly, the astrological pioneers of this invaluable profiling work are unaware of Rudolf Steiner's wisdom.) So anthroposophists are often unaware of the great importance of this work of horoscope interpretation for humanity. A more accurate and valuable profile of a person's psychological nature is not available than that given by an insightful analysis of the natal chart (based on the Inherent Zodiac).

The movement of the planets through the constellational (sidereal) zodiac has no significance for the interpretation of personal natal horoscopes. The tropical (inherent) zodiac is the only valid basis for this; the sidereal zodiac is the wrong zodiac for a natal horoscope. And this is confirmed by Rudolf Steiner directly, as the quote at the beginning of this chapter shows, referring to the tropical or inherent zodiac,

> **"The horoscope which has been cast for thousands of years for the individual, corresponded with infallible exactitude to the four lower parts of the soul..."**

The four lower parts are the physical, etheric astral bodies and earthly ego. He then goes on to say that because humanity is evolving, the horoscope is no longer quite so accurate for the threefold spirit members;[84] but that is not relevant to our discussion. The above quote is not well known, as it is not published in the Complete Works.[85]

But we can note here that the sidereal zodiac is directly relevant to the life-processes of plants and animals, as the bio-dynamic gardeners and farmers well know. It is through the use of such knowledge that this system of farming offers so much more healing and nurturing of the Earth than other organic farming techniques. The wisdom of Rudolf Steiner in regard to agriculture encourages people to develop an awareness of, and make use of, this fact of the influences of the planets through the visible Zodiac.

CONCLUSION

To Rudolf Steiner the Inherent Zodiac is a valid spiritual reality, and the only zodiac to use for a horoscope, for assessment of the soul-qualities of a person. Whereas he regards the Sidereal Zodiac as the correct zodiac for bio-dynamic agricultural activities. It is through using this zodiac that farmers and gardeners not only avoid the use of chemicals harmful to the eco-system, but also uniquely help to nurture the life-forces and elemental realities of the living Earth. The Babylonian BES zodiac is also valid and important, for it is the template, discerned by Babylonian initiates, from which the fourth zodiac, the etheric Cultural Ages zodiac, derives.

Rudolf Steiner gave an invaluable contribution to the work of drawing up a psychological profile of a person, using the Inherent Zodiac. He did this by explaining the nature of our interconnectedness to the planets and the zodiac stars. For more about understanding the horoscope, see the author's *The Horoscope Handbook - a Rudolf Steiner Approach*.

---

[84] That is the Spirit-self, Life-spirit and Spirit-human.
[85] From a lecture on 1st Feb. 1911 in Bonn (archive document).

Appendix Four: Sophia and Anthroposophia

At the inaugural conference for the newly formed Anthroposophical Society, in February 1913, Rudolf Steiner spoke about the word, 'Anthroposophia'. He began by describing how 'Sophia' is an old term for wisdom which arises in the Spiritual-soul, and makes the world, the cosmos that we perceive, much more enlivened and spiritualized. He spoke of how this living quality in the cosmos and in our consciousness was called 'Philosophia' by the Ancient Greek seekers after truth. So with the Greeks, this term was not only a personification of the soul-quality which gives wisdom (including clairvoyance), but also 'Sophia' became a personification, a metaphor, of the **spiritually enlivened cosmos** which this higher consciousness revealed to them. So the word began to have two meanings; neither of which refer to a goddess.. Already in May 1905, Rudolf Steiner spoke of how Dante Alighieri used the figure of his beloved Beatrice, in his book, *the Divine Comedy*, to represent spiritual wisdom (of his times).

Rudolf Steiner told his audience in 1913, of the need to become aware of this spiritually uplifting result of seeking wisdom, of letting wisdom (in Greek, *Sophia*) really be present in the human soul (in Greek, *anthropos*). In this way a new personification of the soul-quality of the wise person and also of the beautifully enlivened cosmos can arise; it is this which the word 'Anthroposophia' expresses. He wanted the audience to really feel a more mature version of the poetic-romantic 'Sophia-Beatrice' idea in regard to the Spiritual-self. He explained that students of anthroposophical wisdom should feel through the spiritualizing of their consciousness, as if a divine reality envelops their soul when anthroposophical wisdom permeates it.[86]

In another lecture, he mentions briefly this idea, but refers directly to Anthroposophy, not the 'Anthroposophia' word, with its poetic associations. He states that "Anthroposophy is, in itself, an invisible human being, which goes around amongst visible human beings".[87] Here we can see that the word 'anthroposophia', derived from the poetic-romantic idea of 'Sophia-Beatrice', is the same as the term 'anthroposophy'. So we can see that in effect, Rudolf Steiner's few, sparse comments on this theme, are urging the insights and astral images flowing into one's consciousness from the Spiritual-self or 'Sophia' state of soul, to be experienced as so alive and enlivening, that one feels as if there were a separate spiritual being-ness all around one.

As he explained on another occasion,

> ...anthroposophy is nothing other than that 'Sophia', that is, that consciousness-content or inwardly experienced element of the human soul, which makes a human being fully a human being...it gives a 'Sophia', that is, a certain kind of consciousness to the soul."[88]

The idea from mystical thinkers in religious and New Age literature, which spreads the attitude that 'Sophia' actually means a goddess, has caused people interested in anthroposophy to come to the conclusion that this same 'goddess' is involved in anthroposophy. However, the existence of such a being is never stated by Rudolf Steiner. As we noted earlier, the only exception is when he refers to the ancient Egyptian religion. But as we saw then, the Egyptian Isis is not about a poetic-romantic goddess, but about three different manifestations of lofty beings, far removed from the mystical yearnings of people in later western cultures. If there were a goddess behind anthroposophy, Rudolf Steiner would have devoted many lectures to such an entity.

Instead, in regard to inspiring beings behind anthroposophy, he referred to the cosmic Christ, to the archangel Michael and also briefly to the archangel Vidar. The least sustainable theories

---

[86] Berlin 3rd Feb. 1913.
[87] GA 158, lect. 16th June 1923.
[88] GA 257, 13th Feb. 1923, p.76.

on this theme are from S. Prokofieff. In his book, *The Heavenly Sophia...* Prokofieff types in a sentence from a lecture of Steiner, so that it says, "Mary was a pure and young **soul**". (p. 123) This implies a 'new soul', or a person who has had only very few lifetimes. Prokofieff then declares that, she was having her first incarnation, just as was Jesus. And hence the (theoretical) 'goddess' Sophia could naturally be expected to overshadow Mary. But the words "quoted" by Prokofieff were never spoken by Steiner.

Steiner's words in the lecture on St. Luke's Gospel directly "quoted" by Prokofieff are, "Mary was a really young **mother**", (i.e., a teen-ager when Jesus was born). Steiner is here referring to her age, and how she **had** to be young, when she gave birth to Jesus, in comparison to the older Mary of St. Matthew's gospel. (Luke Gospel lectures, GA 114, lect. 19th Sept. 1909, p. 108 in German edition). It is valuable to also note here, that Rudolf Steiner taught that Mary (of Luke's Gospel) actually had a {substantial} **number of previous lives** and it was **through the development she underwent during these lives that she became a 'Sophia' or Spirit-Self person**, (Gospel of St. John lecture cycle of 1908, GA 103, lect. 31st May). **So she was an 'old soul', not a young soul.** One has to conclude from this, that the quote from Rudolf Steiner is fictitious, and thoughts underlying *The Heavenly Sophia...*book generally are in contradiction to the clearly stated teachings of Rudolf Steiner.

MITTEILUNGEN

für die Mitglieder der Deutschen Sektion der Theosophischen Gesellschaft

herausgegeben von

MATHILDE SCHOLL.

No. XV.	Cöln, Januar 1913.	No. XV.

Die elfte Generalversammlung der Deutschen Sektion der Theosophischen Gesellschaft findet statt am 2. Februar 1913 in Berlin, im Architektenhause (Saal A) Wilhelmstrasse 92/93. Im Anschluss daran findet eine Versammlung des **Johannesbau-Vereins** statt und eine gesellige Zusammenkunft.

Die erste Generalversammlung der Anthroposophischen Gesellschaft findet ebendaselbst vom 3. bis 7. Febr. 1913 statt.

Ein Brief von Dr. Rudolf Steiner an die Mitglieder der Theosophischen Gesellschaft.

An die Mitglieder der Theosophischen Gesellschaft.

hängnisvoller Art das System Besant innerhalb der Theosophischen Gesellschaft Schule macht. Ich betone ausdrücklich, dass es mir ganz ferne

---

NOTICES

for the members of the German section of the Theosophical Society

published by

Mathilde Scholl

No. 15	**Cologne**, January 1913	No. 15

The 11th AGM of the German Section of the Theosophical Society will take place on 2nd. Feb. 1913, in Berlin in the Architektenhause (hall A), at Wilhemstrasse 92/93. Following on from this there shall be a Meeting of the **St. John's Building Association** and a social gathering.

The First General Conference of the Anthroposophical Society will take place at the same venue from 3rd - 7th Feb. 1913

A Letter from Dr. Rudolf Steiner to the members of the Theosophical Society

---

This original journal from January 1913 announces the founding of the Anthroposophical Society.

**Appendix Five: Aries & The Turning-Point of Time: 1846 BC - AD 1912.
An attempt to unveil the hidden time-cycles and astrological influence
behind the timing of the founding of the Anthroposophical Society in 1912.**

It was on the occasion of the founding of the Anthroposophical Society in 1912 that Rudolf Steiner made available his 1912/13 *Calendar of the Year* and also *The Soul Calendar*. In making the Soul Calendar available, Rudolf Steiner was showing the deep importance to the anthroposophical movement of this new spiritual ecology based on the seasons. With the Calendar and its zodiac graphics, he was indicating the importance of the zodiac in the spiritual life of humanity.

The founding of the Anthroposophical Society occurred in several low-key stages. In 1912, Mathilde Scholl, a personal student of Rudolf Steiner's from Cologne, had suggested that such a society was needed. Consequently, on 28th December in Cologne the new Society was formed, and on the 29th December an evening artistic event was held to celebrate the occasion. In January of 1913, the members of the Theosophical Society in Germany received notice that the first Annual General Meeting of the Anthroposophical Society would take place from the 3rd -7th February, see Illustration 49. So in February of 1913 in Berlin, the new Society was launched into an international social setting. A social vessel to receive the work of Rudolf Steiner had come into existence.

But why did the greatly significant event of the founding of the Anthroposophical Society occur in the year 1912/13? In historical terms, it was due to the scandal of the Theosophical Society's leaders misusing their influential position, to create a fraudulent sensation. They had announced in 1910 that they had found the teenager who was the returned Jesus, the world Messiah. As Rudolf Steiner could point out, this was nonsense, so those Theosophists who had heard and studied Rudolf Steiner's teachings felt that there was a need for a new society to be a vessel of his teachings. But in terms of cosmic cycles of time through which great spiritual powers manifest their influence, why did this event occur in 1912/13? What hidden time-cycle is behind this special year? Exploring this question unveils more of the greatness of the spiritual powers inspiring Rudolf Steiner's activity.

One Cosmic Reason for 1912/13

In the 19th century, the rule of archangel Michael, the Sun Archangel, had begun; this was in 1879, and each such archangelic period of regency lasts for about 340-380 years. Now, the year 1912 is 33 years into this era: the solar number ! Rudolf Steiner taught that the Christ cycle is a 33-year cycle. Jesus Christ lived for 33 years. And we can note here too that King David ruled for 33 years in Jerusalem.

And it is significant too, that the Moon's rhythms are subordinate to this cycle. The lunar monthly cycle is not of the same length of time as the solar month. Every 33 years the lunar and the solar calendars converge. For after 32 years of the lunar synodic months, at the start of the 33rd synodic year, the Moon is at the same position as the sun ! (A lunar synodic month is from the new moon to the next new moon and takes 29.5 days.)

But quite apart from this cycle, were there any forces from the spiritual worlds, connected to the zodiac, and inspired by the cosmic Christ-impulse or the spiritual sun, involved in the emerging of the anthroposophical movement in the flow of historical time i.e., in 1912/13? The answer appears to be, yes there were. Here, we need to consider events in history, from before the Christian era and from after the time of

Christ which according to Rudolf Steiner, have the Mystery of Golgotha as their pivotal point. The most clear example involves two personalities who are normally regarded as purely fictitious, but whom Rudolf Steiner indicates were real, historical people: a hero in the Trojan war, Hector, and a Shakespearean character, prince Hamlet of Denmark. Rudolf Steiner taught that *Hector*, the daring, martial Trojan hero, who lived about 1,200 BC, was reborn after Golgotha as Shakespeare's prince *Hamlet*, the indecisive ditherer. This is obviously a dramatic change, the psychological nature of which Rudolf Steiner did not discuss. The implications of his words here are that Hamlet was an historical character whose inner being had undergone a great change, becoming the reverse or kind of mirror-image of what it had been in the ancient Trojan War. This means that a figure like Hamlet lived about AD 1,200. (Which is a strong reason why Shakespeare's plays are best kept to the original era.)

So why did the anthroposophical impulse emerge in 1912/13 ? What mysterious time cycles are active here ? My research suggests that there exists a deeply sacred cycle of spiritual influences involved here, involving influences from the spiritual sun, active from **before** Golgotha, which are then mirrored **after** Golgotha. A veiled indicator of this was given in Rudolf Steiner's *Calendar of 1912/13.* In addition to the zodiac images, which we have explored, the front cover of Steiner's book contains a very strange illustration; see illustration 50. The graphics here emphasize that the Soul calendar (and the founding of the Anthroposophical Society) occurred 1,879 years after Mystery of Golgotha, which is referred to as "the birth of the ego". This is the number of years after the events of Golgotha which brings us to the year 1912.

So this statement on the front cover points to an historical flow of time, dating history from the Golgotha event, which occurred in AD 33, rather than the birth of Jesus. Now to see the deep mystery in the cosmic timing of the entry of anthroposophy into a human social reality, we need to contemplate this highly esoteric image. On the top of this illustration there are two winged spiritual beings, facing each other as if they are mirror images. But, very significantly, between them is the letter "m", and it forms a kind of barrier between the two upright figures. This letter is like a central area, which divides a left and a right section off from each other.

And of course the letter "m" has in the middle an upright bar, and on the left a bar, and on the right a bar; this also suggests a middle section, which separates off a left and a right side. Furthermore it's important to really note that the two upright winged beings are indeed reflections of each other: that is, they are very similar, but not identical. This is the situation therefore somewhat similar to a mirror-image of anything; the reflection is not a perfect copy of the object; for example, left and right sides are switched around.

So the question here is; of what event, in the past, is the 1912 inauguration of anthroposophy socially, a mirror-image? Firstly, 1912 is strongly highlighted on the cover as being 1,879 years after the Mystery of Golgotha. It was in this year that the social vessel was formed that enables Rudolf Steiner to give the new Christ revelation. For amongst many other things, anthroposophy is the proclamation of the existence of, and the nature of the cosmic Christ, the cosmic sun god known as Osiris in ancient Egypt.

But, if 1912 AD is 1,879 years after the Mystery of Golgotha, to what year BC do we come to, if we go back 1,879 years before AD 33? We arrive at 1846 BC. Remember we are counting from AD 33 the Mystery of Golgotha, not from the birth of Jesus (AD 1). What might have happened then? This takes us back into the 19th century BC. Now, we need to ponder a question: does that unusual upright deity on the right refer to AD

This striking graphic hints at why Anthroposophy emerged
socially in 1912/13 as a reflection of the deeds from 1846 BC.
(The red colouring has been added, AA.)

1912 and the left one to 1846 BC? And as a small detail emphasising this, does the right bar of the letter "m" refer to AD 1912, and the left bar to 1846 BC ?

In anthroposophy, and for many theologians, the nineteenth cent BC is the century, when the great patriarch Abraham (or Abram) lived, the founder of the tribal nation of the Hebrews. What has the life of Abraham to do with the spiritual Sun, or with Christ ? It was his destiny to establish the Hebrew nation, the Israelites, amongst whom the human vessel of the Cosmic Sun-god would be born, Jesus of Nazareth. And then the Mystery of Golgotha could occur, leading to a permeating of the Earth's aura with the spiritual forces of the sun-god Christ.

Abraham was a Babylonian man, from the city of Ur in Chaldea, situated on the banks of the Tigris River. He migrated north-west to Haran in Canaan, and then later into Egypt. One deeply significant esoteric event in his life, concerns his encounter with the very significant spiritual being Melchizedek, known from Atlantean times. Melchizedek is not a human being, he is as Rudolf Steiner taught, an spirit being, and thus "one aeon ahead of humanity" (as stated in an unpublished lecture). In other words he is an Angel, and we may assume, a very advanced Angel. For this spirit being, Melchizedek, was the leader of the Atlantean sun mysteries, and as such he is a representative of the sun god, the cosmic Christ.[89] Of this meeting the Bible says in Genesis 14:17;

> After Abram returned from defeating Kedorlaomer and the kings allied with him, the king of Sodom came out to meet him in the Valley of Shaveh {that is, the King's Valley}. Then Melchizedek, king of Salem brought out bread and wine. He was a priest of God Most High...and Melchizedek blessed Abram, saying, "Blessed be Abram by God Most High, Creator of heaven and earth. And blessed be God Most High, who delivered your enemies into your hands".

Abraham's mission was to start the new tribal Semitic group, the Hebrew people, who were destined to be the ancestors of Jesus, the man who is to be vessel of the descending Sun God, Jesus of Nazareth. We shall consider the symbolic significance of the bread and wine later. Without this involvement of Abraham there would have been, in effect, no Mystery of Golgotha, as the ancient Hebrews would not have come into being.

When did this meeting take place? Bible scholars are unsure. There have been many suggestions as to Abraham's precise chronology, because the Bible does not give exact historical data. But the dates most often mentioned are in the 19th century BC, such as 1876, 1875, and 1860. As we shall see, from what is indicated by the graphics in the Calendar, this meeting probably occurred in 1846 BC. Let's see what Rudolf Steiner says about this encounter,

> "This meeting of Abraham with Melchizedek is a meeting of the greatest, most universal significance...he communicated to Abraham the secret of the Sun sphere..."[90]

Thus Melchizedek, as a representative of the Cosmic Christ, was in effect attuning Abraham to the future deed of Christ and thus of humanity's spiritual redemption. He was preparing Abraham for the momentous task of bringing the nation of Israel into being. Furthermore, Rudolf Steiner also affirms the general Biblical tradition that the Archangel Michael was the Folk-Spirit of the ancient Hebrews, at least for some

---

[89] Rudolf Steiner, *The Gospel of St. Matthew*, GA 123, lect. 4th Sept 1910.
[90] ibid.

centuries. And thus the mission of Abraham can also be brought into connection with this great sun archangel.[91]

So Abraham was a servant of Michael, and we can also say this is true of Rudolf Steiner, and in terms of anthroposophical knowledge, we can say that Abraham was a servant of the sun god, as was Rudolf Steiner. We need to briefly note here that Rudolf Steiner tells us that in the 19th century BC, there began a gradual closing down of the sensing of the higher worlds. This was a condition which caused a loss of inner feeling for the truth of reincarnation and karma.

And what was so special about Abraham ? Rudolf Steiner explained that he was "the first human being to have a capacity to {intuitively} think about the Divine with physical-brain consciousness"[92] that is, whilst living in the physical body. Whereas with other people, (in earlier times and still in his time too), such a perception required attaining the state of 'psychic-image consciousness' (or 'Imagination') by activating clairvoyant-psychic abilities. Abraham did not need that, as he was pioneering the ability to intuit and conceptualize such truths.[93] As we shall soon see, this implies that Abraham was working with energies from Aries, the zodiac influence which governs our thinking life and the brain.

Consequently the Hebrew tribes would be leading this process of moving on a path towards closing down the holistic higher consciousness and the development of the earthly ego-sense. For this reason, Melchizedek inaugurated the ritualistic sacred meal of bread and wine, a ritual which, after many centuries of Judaism as established by Moses, became echoed in the Christian sacrament of the Last Supper. This sacrament is, as Rudolf Steiner taught, anticipating the ritual use of bread and wine in the Last Supper. This is about sanctifying daily life for a no-longer-directly-clairvoyant people, by pragmatically linking daily life, and nutrition in fluid and solid matter, to the divine.

And now we can see that with the founding of the Anthroposophical Society in AD 1912 that there came about a reflection of the mission of Abraham ! For in 1912 through Rudolf Steiner, the greatest revelations in our culture about the cosmic Christ and the fact of the descent of the Christ long ago, were made available. The mirror image of this occurred in 1846 BC, when Melchizedek met Abraham and prepared him to establish an ethnic group for service to a **future** sacred goal: the descent of the sun god to the Earth. Thus when in 1912 a social form was created to allow Rudolf Steiner to present the nature of Christ to humanity, and to proclaim the etheric reappearing of Jesus, that established a basis for people to receive the teachings of Rudolf Steiner. And this was a reflection of what was the mission of Abraham.

A core element in anthroposophy is a connection to the momentous **past** events of Golgotha and hence also to the Spiritual Sun. Anthroposophy looks back to Golgotha as a given fact, and gives guidance as to how to form a connection to the Christ Mysteries for the future. These mysteries are no doubt, in various ways, a metamorphosis of those Mysteries which Melchizedek once reigned over, in the hallowed halls of the Atlantean temple dedicated to the sun oracle. This momentous inception of the mission of Abraham began when Melchizedek met him, and so I am suggesting that this occurred in 1846 BC.

---

[91] GA 265, p. 407.
[92] GA 123, pages 68-70, lecture, 4th Sept. 1910.
[93] See for example, ref. 80 and his lectures "the Deeper Secrets of Human Evolution in the light of the Gospels, (GA 117) lects. 9th Nov. 1909, 14th Nov. 1909 and 19th Nov. 1909.

And now again to the graphics on the cover page of the Calendar 1912/13 with the two spiritual beings facing each other, as if reflecting each other. The letter 'm' between them, together with the large numbers 1879, seem to indicate that the above conclusions are correct; Abraham in 1846 BC and Rudolf Steiner in AD 1912. But there is another indicator on this cover, affirming my conclusions; this involves the zodiacal wisdom of the Mesopotamian era, which is the era of Abraham.

In the Book of Genesis it is told how, some years after being given his mission by Melchizedek, Abraham faces another potent spiritual trial; he is called upon to apparently sacrifice his own son, Isaac. But in fact, his God stops him and Abraham sacrifices a ram or lamb on the altar to God instead of his son, thereby sealing his commitment to God, described as "renewing his covenant with God".

I suggest that this event very probably occurred some 19 years after 1846 BC; that is, in the year 1827 BC. For in that year on the spring equinox day, the sun entered the sign of Aries the Ram – but in the sectors of the ancient Babylonian Equal-sized Sectors zodiac, (or the 'BES zodiac'), not in the etheric zodiac used in anthroposophy, as the basis of the zodiacal cultural Ages, see Illustration 51. Earlier, we examined this ancient Babylonian zodiac and saw how it indirectly provides the basis of the Cultural Ages in anthroposophical teachings in Appendix Two. It is significant that 19 years is one lunar nodal cycle; so here in this pivotal trial for Abraham, the lunar energies are being integrated into the greater solar influences. That in this case it is the BES zodiac which is significant, may be due to the fact that, as Rudolf Steiner emphasizes, the especial ability of Abraham was caused by a subtle change in his physical body.[94] Sidereal influences do have an impact in the physical world.

Now looking again at the front page of the Calendar of 1912, we see the sign of Aries (in red) placed in this image. Why is this symbol important ? Because Rudolf Steiner also revealed that this incident of Abraham sacrificing a lamb instead of his son Isaac, has a hidden esoteric zodiacal significance. It is a veiled way of saying that Abraham was **working with the faculty of human cognition**. That is, with Aries forces, which enable the perceiving of either the sense world or spiritual realms. It is Aries that governs the forehead, which means, as we have seen, it was through the Aries forces that our frontal lobe was developed. It is through this area of the brain that we experience our ideas.[95] So behind the story of Abraham substituting a lamb is veiled, for those with ears to hear, the great zodiacal task of Abraham to respond in a new and special way to the influence of Aries energies.

He was to turn away from the age-old clairvoyance, and to conceptualize spiritual truths, rather than have astral images appear. Hence Rudolf Steiner taught of Abraham, that he was "the only human being of his times to have a capacity to sense the divine with physical-brain consciousness as concepts."[96] For anthroposophically, as we see in the Aries image of the Stuttgart ceiling, the influence of Aries is about cognition of either the sense world or the spiritual realms. Abraham was also capable of some clairvoyant experiences, as the Bible records, but Rudolf Steiner here is emphasizing that it was primarily his sensitivity to (or subtle awareness of) the spiritual without leaving his normal earthly consciousness, that he was pioneering. It is for this reason that this great man (and of course all the other saints) was repeatedly called "a man of faith". For example, "By faith, Abraham, when he was called to go to a place that he would later receive as his inheritance {the Promised Land}, obeyed and went,…" (Hebrews, 11:8).

---

[94] GA 123, lect. 3rd September, 1910.
[95] GA 117, lect. 9th Nov. 1909.
[96] GA 117 lects. 14th Nov. 1909 & 19th Nov. 1909.

How the chronology of Abraham's life would now appear:

Abraham was born in 1926 BC, so that:
* in 1851 BC he goes to Canaan at 75 years of age, and thus:
* in **1846** BC **he meets with Melchizedek**, at 80 yrs of age (1,879 years before Golgotha)
* in ca.1843 BC, has a spiritual experience, results in a covenant with the Lord (Gen 15:12)
* in 1840, is 86 years old: the Mamre oak experience occurs and he then fathers Ishmael
* in 1827, is 99 yrs old: prepares to sacrifice Isaac, but instead a lamb is used; this deed 'renews his covenant' with the Lord, but also inaugurates the process of him using Aries forces in his consciousness (Gen. 22) We can note that 99 is 3 x 33; a triple solar number.

We need to pause here to understand something of great significance for biblical studies, and that is that the term, 'faith', like some others from the New Testament (and other old texts) have lost their original meaning. The actual meaning of the term today is incorrect to what it meant in ancient times; it had been replaced with an intellectual substitute. The most common exhortations of the priesthood in earlier times, was "to have faith". If someone ceased to be involved in the church, it was said that they had "lost their faith". The following teaching of Rudolf Steiner explains the situation,

> Faith as it originally was understood, referred to the quality of **not weakening the inherent spiritual reality of something that we come across, {especially for the first time}, by that which we are.**.[97]

That is, what our inner being (e.g., intellectual analytical processes) brings towards the perceived object should not weaken our soul's sensing of what that thing really is.

This trial in the life of Abraham involving his son Isaac, also means that in 1827 BC, the 'people of the Lamb of God' were brought into being by the deed of Abraham. For then Isaac would be able to stay alive, and later father his own children, and thus the nation of Israel would come into being. And it was in that year, as we noted above, the sun entered the sign of Aries – in the Babylonian Equal-sized Sectors zodiac, or the 'BES zodiac'.

Thus, 1,879 years before Golgotha (in 1846 BC) there existed Abraham, who was grasping sacred truths via his thinking, that is, his awareness as an incarnate person, amidst an environment in which the Mysteries were to start gradually losing their power. And then 1,879 years after Golgotha (in AD 1912) there came Rudolf Steiner, grasping sacred truths about the sun god with a new clairvoyance. And inspired by the Christ and those divine beings who assist the Christ-impulse, in particular, the archangels Michael and Vidar. But, here we can recall that in a private conversation Rudolf Steiner explained that he himself was the only initiate with the ability of seeing into spiritual worlds who was also able to present those truths to others *in conceptual form.* And it was an essential part of his work, to bring a profound clarity and depth to the idea of reincarnation and karma, as a way to re-establish the Mysteries. At least to make a beginning in this work, amongst the no longer holistically aware modern human beings.

This is the exact reversal, indeed a type of mirror-image, of Abraham's task, and a reversal of the spiritual-cultural dynamics of that time. Rudolf Steiner was working with seership Aries forces in a new and powerful way. So in the post-Golgotha era, the Christ-impulse of anthroposophy in AD 1912 helps people to relate to the Sun mysteries, and to create a path to the higher consciousness of the Spiritual-self. This is **in contrast to** the dynamics in 1846 BC, when Abraham was preparing to work with the

---

[97] R Steiner Lect 7/Dec/'05 In G/A 54 untranslated.

closing down of the old holistic awareness and the awakening to the earthly ego. So, in 1846 BC, Abraham, helped by the Christ herald, Melchizedek, and we can conclude, the archangel Michael, created the basis for a 'chosen people' of the Christ-impulse. But in 1912 AD Rudolf Steiner, helped by the Archangel Michael, and Archangel Vidar, and other divine beings, created the basis for a new community, which one could regard as part of a new 'chosen people': that is, those souls who feel the need to become people belonging to the Christ-impulse.

For from Rudolf Steiner's work, Anthroposophy is now read and put into practice, and thus uniting people world-wide through deeds; and through this activity people are developing an inner bond to each other. This happens because of these people's mutual reverence for, and consciousness of, these spiritual truths, regardless of their religious or national boundaries. This is, in effect, a new global community of the spirit.

So in Anthroposophy, Rudolf Steiner created a new community of human beings, in harmony with the spirit (or, a cosmopolitan view of Christ as the sun god). And finally, as a further example of this 'mirroring' activity, Rudolf Steiner tells us, in a lecture on the nature of the Reappearing of Jesus, that the initiate Abraham would also become active, helping to inspire humanity in regard to being aware of the Reappearance of Jesus Christ.[98]

Anthroposophy responds to and reflects in a new way, the sacrament established by Melchizedek. As Rudolf Steiner taught, the bread symbolizes the spiritual which comes to us from outside. And the wine symbolizes the spiritual which arises from within us. Hence those who eventually take up esoteric meditative striving no longer need the religious ritual.

These are, it seems, the hidden zodiacal truths behind the striking image placed on the front cover of The Calendar of 1912/13.

---

[98] Rudolf Steiner, lect.25th Jan 1910, *The Event of the Reappearing of Christ in the Ethers* (GA 118).

51 The turning point of time: 1912-13 as a mirror-image of 1846 BC

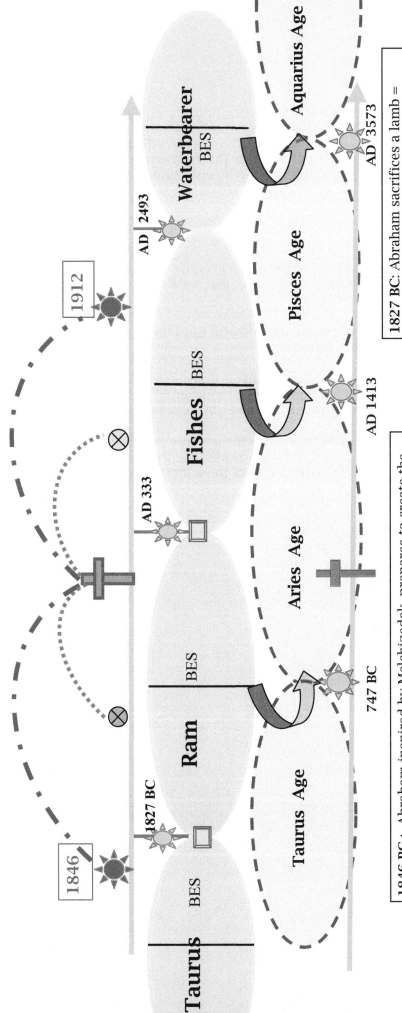

Taurus BES

Ram | BES

Fishes | BES

Waterbearer BES

Taurus Age

Aries Age

Pisces Age

Aquarius Age

1846

1827 BC

AD 333

1912

AD 2493

AD 333

AD 1413

747 BC

AD 3573

1846 BC : Abraham inspired by Melchizedek, prepares to create the 12 tribes to enable the Messiah to be born & bring the Christ-being into the Earth's aura.

AD 1912-13 : Rudolf Steiner's anthroposophical impulse strives to form a global community of renewal from the cosmic Christ-impulse.

1827 BC: Abraham sacrifices a lamb = Aries forces used to cognize by intuition, not by the old clairvoyance; as the sun enters Aries, in the "BES" zodiac

AD 333: in Greco-Latin people the inner feeling developed that divine beings are irrelevant; as sun enters Pisces in the "BES" zodiac

about 1200 BC: Hector & about AD 1200: Hamlet

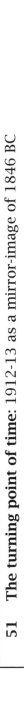

In Conclusion

We have been able to undertake a wonderful journey into the zodiac, perhaps re-awakening feelings that we had when we first looked at old imaginative drawings of the constellations in our childhood. We have been able to contemplate those extraordinary images from the lost zodiac in Stuttgart, telling us about the influence of the zodiac in human evolving. We have been able to clarify our understanding of this zodiac by comparing its images to the drawings published in the Calendar of 1912/13.

We have discovered that the "Twelve Moods" are actually invaluable meditations on the spiritual psychology of the sun-signs.

We have seen that Rudolf Steiner taught that the Tropical zodiac, or Inherent zodiac, is the only zodiac system to use when drawing up a horoscope; and we have noted various examples of how Rudolf Steiner validated this zodiac.

We have discovered the mysterious basis of the zodiacal Cultural Ages that form the basis of the anthroposophical view of the flow of history.

Finally, we considered some evidence for the zodiacal and time-cycle influences operative in bringing about a social vessel for the emergence of anthroposophy in 1912/13, and how this is a reflection in the flow of time, of the appearance of Melchizedek to Abraham.

May these inner 'zodiacal journeyings' help to serve the purpose that led Rudolf Steiner to offer these treasures to people in modern times, which was possible through the dedicated effort of Imma von Eckhardtstein, who painted or drew many of these images.

GLOSSARY of some central anthroposophical terms

aeon: a long evolutionary time. There are seven of these, and we are now in the fourth such epoch. They are the Saturn, Sun, Moon, Earth (which has two halves, Mars and Mercury) Jupiter, Venus and Vulcan aeons.

Ahriman: an evil entity responsible for the attitude which sees matter as the only thing in creation, denying spiritual reality. It correlates to the Biblical term, Satan.

Angels: spiritual beings who are one aeon ahead of human beings in the evolution.

anthroposophy: a Greek word that literally means 'human soul wisdom'. In Rudolf Steiner's usage it means the wisdom that can dawn in a person's consciousness in their spiritual-soul; and which fully manifests when the Spirit-self is developed.

archangels: spiritual beings who are two aeons ahead of human beings in the evolution.

astral body: the soul, seen as an aura around the body.

astral realm: the Soul-world or soul realms, above the ethers, but below the Devachanic realms.

astrality: soul energies, but often it refers mainly to the feelings.

BES: the Babylonian Equal-sized Segments zodiac.

Cosmic Christ: the highest of the 'Powers' or sun-gods.

Devachan: the true heavens above the Soul-world; a Theosophical term from the Sanskrit meaning 'realm of the shining gods'; it is the realm of the archetypal Idea, of Plato.

the Double: a term usually referring to the Lower Self.

ego or self or I: the sense of self, but the eternal self is linked to this. Hence the ego is a dual or twofold thing.

egoism or egoistic: not quite the same as the well-known term egotism (which means conceit). Egoism is used by Rudolf Steiner to mean either the state of having a normal earth-centred ego, or for this earthly sense of self behaving in a selfish way.

etheric body: is made of the four ethers and duplicates the physical body's appearance, from which organic matter, such as new cells, are condensed.

ethers: subtle energies which sustain all living things on the Earth. Electricity and magnetism are formed as they decompose.

Group-soul: a spirit-being to whom all the animals of a particular species belong.

intellectual-soul: the rational, logical capacity.

intuitive-soul: (see spiritual-soul)

Imagination, Inspiration, Intuition: Latin words for the three types of clairvoyance, but which mean something different in everyday usage in English to the meanings that Rudolf Steiner gives them.

Imagination: the first stage of clairvoyance: this can be called 'psychic-image consciousness' as it is when astral or etheric images are perceived, (in normal English usually means 'fantasy'.)

Imaginations: astral thought-forms.

Inspiration: this can be called 'cosmic-spiritual consciousness', perceiving or 'breathing-in' wisdom, from lower Devachan. (In normal English usually means a strongly felt creative urge or idea.)

Intuition: this can be called a 'high initiation consciousness'. It is a perceiving or inwardly becoming one with another being. This state allows the seer to perceive at an upper Devachan level. (In normal English usually means a semi- psychic awareness of something.)

intuition: can be used by Rudolf Steiner for the above high seership, but can sometimes appear in English anthroposophical texts in its usual English meaning of 'insights' (translating such German words as 'ahnen').

life-force: an alternative term for ether.

life-force organism: the ether body.

Life-spirit: the divinized etheric body, is made of Devachanic energies.

lower-self: the soul qualities that are tainted with Luciferic or Ahrimanic influences. It can be thought of as threefold, the lower thinking, feeling and will. But Rudolf Steiner also described it as sevenfold, being the lower qualities of the seven classical planets in astrology.

Lucifer: a 'fallen' entity who opposes the intentions of the higher gods, creating an ungrounded, naïve attitude, but also instils a sense of self and enthusiasm for beauty, art and sensuality.

sentient-soul: the feelings, emotion (aspect) of the soul.

soul: appears as an aura, and contains the sentient-soul, intellectual-soul and spiritual-soul.

Spirit-human: the divine forces underlying the physical body, present in our subconscious will.

Spirit-self: the result of the purified and enlightened threefold soul-body or astral body.

spiritual-soul: also translated as 'consciousness soul', and could be called the intuitive soul. This is the soul capacity which underlies intuitive decision-making or intuitive flashes of insight. But it is also the most individualized or 'ego-ic' soul capacity, and can tend towards a hardened self-centredness.

Spiritual-sun: the sun on its soul (or astral) level, behind the physical globe, and also on its actual spiritual level (also referred to as the Devachanic level): these levels comprise many energies and divine beings.

thinking: can be used to mean the exercise of our intelligence, but it is also used to mean any of the three clairvoyant states we can attain.

INDEX

Illustration acknowledgments

1- 5: From the Stuttgart ceiling photo of ca. 1913
6: the author
7 - 19: as for 1- 5
20 - 32: from the Calendar 1912/13
33 - 35: from the Goetheanum window
36: from the Triptych Grail by Anna May, photo 1913 used in a poster, 1975
37 - 43: the author
44: from the Calendar 1912/13
45 - 48: the author
49: Journal of the German branch of the Theosophical Society, 1913
50: from The Calendar 1912/13
51: the author
End-page: black/white photos, published in *Sternkalender* 1947, Vlg. von A. Vogel, Winterthur, Switzerland.

Also:
37, 39 - 43: Background photos of the heavens are from NASA Space agency; namely DEL 252: see, www.nasa.gov/multimedia/imagegallery. The use of these graphics does not imply that the owner of these graphics in anyway endorses the worldview expressed in this book.

47 & 48 For the two horoscopes of the albino people, I used the excellent Astrodeluxe Software of John Halloran (http:// www.halloran.com). The use of these graphics does not imply that the owner of these graphics in anyway endorses the worldview expressed in this book.

Zodiac sigils
These are from: http://www.fontspace.com/category/greek,zodiac,symbols. The use of these graphics does not imply that the owner of these graphics in anyway endorses the worldview expressed in this book.

Also by this author:

Living a Spiritual Year: seasonal festivals in both hemispheres (1992, new edition 2016)
The Way to the Sacred   (2003)
The Foundation Stone Meditation: a new commentary (2005)
Dramatic Anthroposophy: Identification and contextualization of primary features
  of Rudolf Steiner's anthroposophy. (Ph.D. thesis, Otago University, 2005)
Two Gems from Rudolf Steiner   (2014)
The Hellenistic Mysteries & Christianity   (2014)
Rudolf Steiner Handbook   (2014)
Horoscope Handbook - a Rudolf Steiner Approach (2015)
The Meaning of the Goetheanum Windows (2016)

See also Damien Pryor:

The nature & origin of the Tropical Zodiac
Stonehenge
The Externsteine
Lalibela
The Great Pyramid & the Sphinx

website: www.rudolfsteinerstudies.com

ART PRINTS AND POSTERS
A selection of art prints and diagrams illustrating Rudolf Steiner's anthroposophy
is available through a link on the author's website; including the lost Stuttgart Zodiac

The original black–white photos of the Stuttgart zodiac, from ca, 1915.

CPSIA information can be obtained
at www.ICGtesting.com
Printed in the USA
BVOW10*0238081016

4683BVAU00001B/1/P